THERE'S LIGHT

ARTWORKS AND CONVERSATIONS EXAMINING BLACK MASCULINITY, IDENTITY AND MENTAL WELL-BEING

GLENN LUTZ

THERE'S LIGHT: Artworks & Conversations
Examining Black Masculinity, Identity & Mental Well-being.

www.theres-light.com

Published by LIORAFFE, in collaboration with Glenn Lutz Studio.

www.lioraffe.com

You can follow Glenn Lutz's work at www.glennlutz.com and on
Instagram at @glenn_lutz.

Author: Glenn Lutz
Development Editor: Aaliyah Cotton
Editors: Lyric Dodson & Kathleen St. Louis Caliento, Ph.D.
Cover Design & Interior Layout: PAPRIKA

FOR US Edition, 2022.

Printed in The United States of America

ISBN 9780578327532

LIORAFFE   glenn lutz studio

THE SKY COULD FALL DOWN,
THE WIND COULD CRY NOW.
THE STRONG IN ME,
I STILL SMILE.

– KENDRICK LAMAR

FOR

US

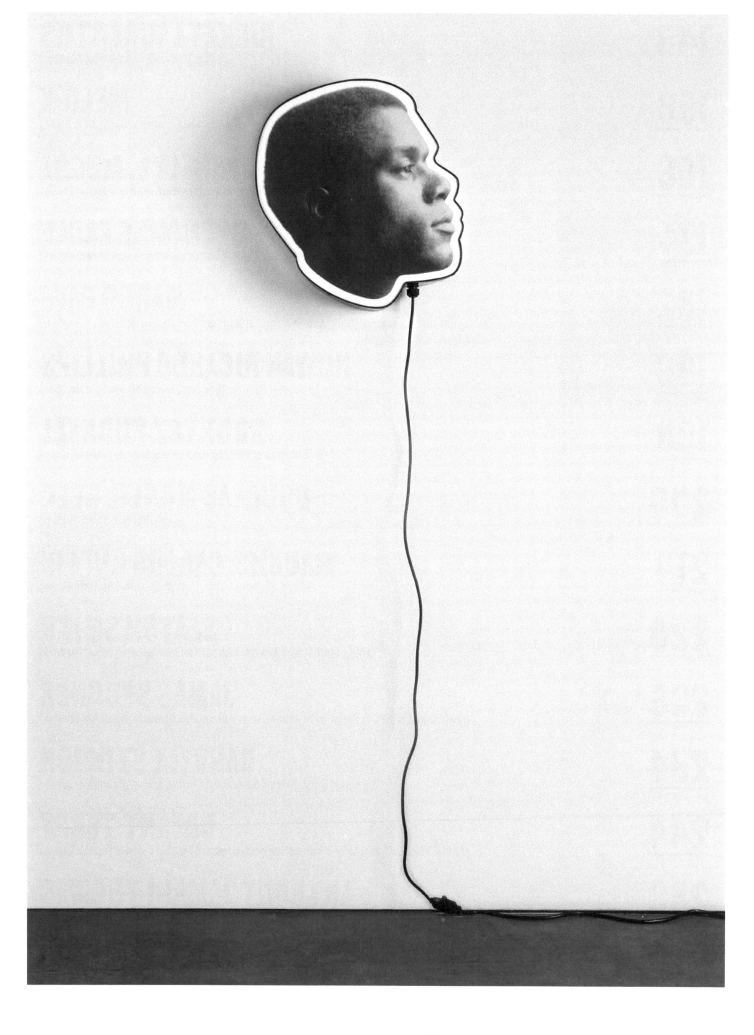

PREFACE
BY
GLENN LUTZ

Like many of my peers growing up outside of Los Angeles in the early 2000s, I found life complicated. My teenage years were a dizzying mix of Boy Scouts, graffiti art, fighting, performing in television commercials, drugs, skateboarding, womanizing, spelling bee championships, and a food and cigarette addiction that would be an issue in my life for years to come. I was also wrestling with anxiety, depression, Obsessive-Compulsive Disorder, and an undiagnosed bipolar disorder. I internalized pent-up frustration, struggled with emotions like guilt, shame, and paranoia, and had a skewed view of what it meant to be a man. I went to five different high schools in four years, including a military school and a boarding school in rural Missouri. The self-medicating I grew accustomed to almost killed me a few times, with one of the closest calls being an alcohol overdose at the age of fifteen. One of my lowest rock bottom moments was landing in a psychiatric ward after a botched suicide attempt at sixteen. In the midst of all of that, I had loving parents, support from family, and friends who were concerned about me. I also had a guiding light inside me that was sure I was more than my emotions or circumstances. I knew deep down that life was worth living.

Looking back, I can see how I struggled to be my authentic self and ignored my traumas, fears, and mental health. I had faced a health crisis, witnessed abuse and violence, and often found myself in dangerous situations. I was insecure about being biracial and felt like I wasn't black enough, being the son of a Haitian and Cuban mother and a white, German and Dutch father. I was obsessed with the Christian, biblical apocalypse and had a lot of existential questions due to my religious upbringing. I felt insecure about my spiritual beliefs, as my father was a Presbyterian minister and theologian. I was trying to figure out who I was and unsure who I wanted to be. I can't count all the times I got harassed by police officers, judged by teachers, or followed around a store by security guards, simply because I'm Black. I had dreams and ambitions clouded by a need for real love. I was searching for that kind of love, as opposed to the fake, transactional one that's predicated on status, money, physical appearances, and accomplishments. It would take a divorce and moving back in with my parents to realize that real love starts from within and that I can't love anyone until I love myself.

My story isn't unique, and we've all had our fair share of tough times. I've found that counseling and examining life through art have been the most fulfilling therapies for me. The approach to my art practice is heavily inspired by the conceptual artist Sol Lewitt's statement that "The idea becomes a machine that makes the art." In this case, the idea that shaped There's Light was a question: "What does it look like when Black men come together to open up and share their experiences, with the intention of personal and collective healing?" That question led to a more interpretive dissection of Lewitt's idea and posed the question, "What if we apply this model to our minds, in that we can become a 'machine that makes,' creating light and abundance in our own lives?" Not through magical thinking, blind optimism, or a get rich quick scheme, but through self-love, mindfulness, gratitude, and working towards something meaningful in these dark times.

These last couple of years have been rough. We're still in the thick of it, and the loss, isolation, injustice, and stress we've all experienced have affected us in ways that we still don't fully understand. It's forced so many of us to take an honest look at where we're at mentally. I truly believe that art is a critical framework to examine our shared and individual experiences. I also think that the best way for art to be genuinely universal is to be culturally specific. There's Light was created for us, Black men, but there's something within its pages for everyone. I didn't set out to exclude Black women or other people from this exercise. Instead, I focused specifically on Black masculinity while unpacking the realities and myths surrounding it and how we can achieve mental wellness amidst it all. I also don't think mental well-being is some puritanical utopia, and personally would never want it to be. Life is complex, and there's beauty in the highs and lows. I believe mental wellness is about loving oneself in every moment, accepting oneself fully, living with a growth mindset, and finding personal success by living life on one's terms. So, even though the narratives within these pages are unique and distinct, they are altogether human. At our core lies a universality that we all share.

There's Light contains our convictions, pains, joys, and work, but ultimately it presents our stories. We tell stories for many reasons. Sometimes we tell them to argue a point, and sometimes we tell them to share a lesson. Most importantly, we tell stories to communicate a feeling. We tell them to say, "This is my experience, and this is how it felt. Do you feel me? Can you relate? Is it inspiring? Did you go through something similar?" I've found that in life, we have more in common with each other than we often think.

AT OUR CORE LIES A UNIVERSALITY THAT WE ALL SHARE

33

JEFFREY ALLEN

GLENN You're the co-founder of C.A.R.E. Inc., and you also provide counseling services to elementary-age children. Can you speak about your practice, what you do on a daily basis, and the importance of therapy for that age group?

JEFFREY I work for a community mental health agency, and am assigned to serve in a particular elementary school. I provide counseling services within the school, free of charge, and am available to service any and all children with Medi-Cal. In my practice, I mainly focus on child psychotherapy and family therapy. I also educate parents and teachers, and advocate for children's rights. I provide what we call "rehab support" with a lot of skill-building as well, so I am fortunate that my site has additional funding sources that allow me to expand my scope so I'm not just focused on children.

Through the counseling program, I've facilitated social skills and emotional support groups, both inside and outside of the school system. We also offer activities for the children during the summer and winter breaks and do our best to engage them in things they aren't typically exposed to. We take every opportunity to expand their horizons and introduce them to new experiences.

G One thing you've spoken about is your desire to become a registered play therapist. Can you speak about this style of therapy and why you believe it's important?

J My specialty area is diversified in terms of age, but I'm specifically interested in working with two-year-olds. The essence of Play Therapy is that play is the language of children. They express themselves through their behavior, and oftentimes, play is the vehicle. Those behaviors can be free or expressive. Through Play Therapy, we utilize play to support them and help them navigate their emotions since they're unable to verbally communicate. Take, for example, the little girl at home playing with her dolls. She may have a mommy and daddy doll and cause them to argue, expressing that her parents fight often. She's trying to make sense of the world and does that through play.

As a play therapist, I'm able to observe them and even engage in it to help them process what's happening, whether consciously or subconsciously. Our goal is to provide them with a free space and encourage them to explore, creating a cathartic experience. We then accompany the play with skill-building, breathing techniques, and psychoeducation.

G In your line of work, are you seeing any specific themes or trends, specifically among children of color in the school you work at?

J Absolutely. Through my observations, I've witnessed the often complex, traumatic experiences a lot of children are dealing with, whether it's living in a dangerous neighborhood or being subject to things they should not have to witness. It's a part of their reality, so anxiety and posttraumatic stress disorder are often present. Even though these kids are often diagnosed with ADHD (Attention-deficit/hyperactivity disorder) or ODD (Oppositional defiant disorder), their behavioral issues usually stem from unresolved trauma.

G Can you speak about your work as a behavior interventionist and how you approached the practice?

J Well, there are two parts. The behavior interventionist work I did was not psycho-based; it was very behavioral in nature, very Pavlov, "train the dog to punch the bell." I'm into teaching kids that their actions will have consequences. We want to increase their positive actions, so they get more positive consequences.

Let's say the child has anxiety about an upcoming school performance or reading aloud in class. To cope with their anxiety, they might act out and perform a lot of attention-seeking actions. In therapy, we take the time to explore and process why that's an issue for them, where the anxiety stemmed from, and how to respond if it arises again. If the child responds through verbal communication, they get rewarded. It can be a verbal affirmation or a small sticker, and as time progresses, we build up to greater rewards.

The therapeutic work I do explores the messaging a child is getting about themselves and how that messaging is affecting their behavior. For example, if a child receives a message that they're not good, not worthy, not smart, not beautiful, or any combination of those things, they may seek attention and cry out for help. If they struggle with math, they may think they're not that smart, so when it comes time to do math work, they all of a sudden go off the rails. My practice helps them process those emotions and assists them in understanding why those messages are not true. We aim to reframe their thinking and affect positive change.

G Do you think there is enough support for kids and are you optimistic that this level of therapy is happening in all schools across the county?

CHILDREN **ARE** **TREATED** **AS** **THIS** **UNSEEN** **AND** **UNHEARD** **PORTION** **OF** **THE** **POPULATION,** **A** **GROUP** **OF** **PEOPLE** **WITHOUT** **RIGHTS** **OR** **ANY** **ENCOURAGEMENT** **TO** **SPEAK** **OUT,** **BUT** **STILL, WE EXPECT THEM** **TO BECOME** **ADULTS** **AND** **THRIVE** **IN** **THIS** **WORLD.**

J There's a lack of support, even with all of the extensive work we do. I think what oftentimes is not discussed is that resources are typically available for kids on the far ends of the spectrum, behaviorally and financially. There's a demographic of people who don't make a lot of money but make just enough to not be considered impoverished, and their kids often get left out. There needs to be a holistic system of helping all children. You shouldn't have to be dirt poor or filthy rich to receive services. Everyone should be able to get the support they need.

G What brought you to the profession?

J I fell in love with a psychology course I took in high school. By the time I got to college, I knew what my major would be. After taking some courses, I realized there were so many fields, such as marriage therapy, family therapy, and child therapy, which I deeply connected with because of my childhood. I remember being a kid, crying out for help, and not having those cries heard.

I began to learn more about child therapy in particular and knew I wanted to be a champion and an advocate for kids who were struggling. What can we do to support them through tough situations?

I believe America needs to truly love our children. Our country, our states, and our citizens really need to appreciate these young lives. In this country, children are treated as this unseen and unheard portion of the population, a group of people without rights or any encouragement to speak out, but still, we expect them to become adults and thrive in this world. There's a lot of energy around the expectations we place on kids, and yet, they're often failed every step of the way, whether it is in education, lunch and nutrition, or access to physical, visual, or performing arts. We don't give kids what they need, but we still expect them to be successful. It's kind of amazing that American adults even operate at the level they're able to.

I believe we need to talk to our kids more and figure out what they want to learn and what they need to thrive. They are going to become the adults who prescribe you medicine, work in your office, or run for president. Let's be clear: Donald Trump was once a child. He was also an innocent child, to a degree, until he was influenced by his environment. The same goes for Dr. Martin Luther King, Jr. They were all children, so a lot of what they were fed in their formative years dictated who they became as adults. I believe that if we keep that in mind, we can begin to create a society that has prosperous future generations instead of broken, hateful, and angry ones.

KYLE D. JORDAN

Pg. 41
Little Boy Blue, 2019
© Kyle D. Jordan.
Courtesy of the artist

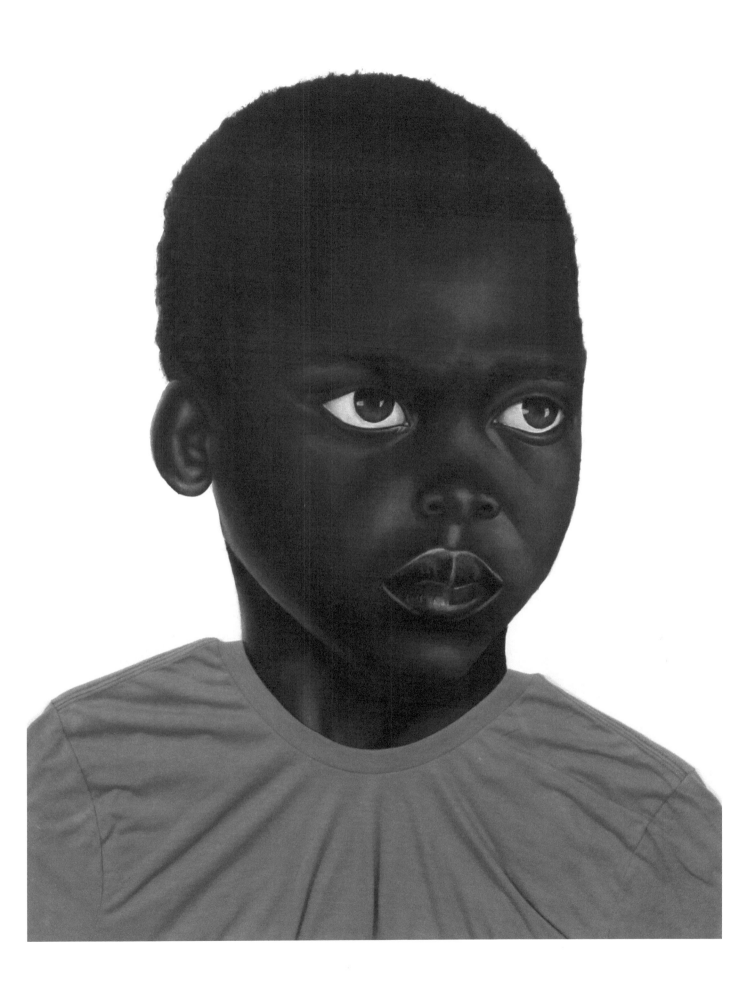

"UG
BRAN

BRANDON

LY
DON"

CARLTON

GLENN You go by the moniker Ugly Brandon, with UGLY standing for "U Gotta Love Yourself." Can you speak about the origin of that nickname and what inspired that phrase?

BRANDON Growing up, I wasn't bullied or anything like that. I just dealt with the homies teasing me and calling me ugly to clown me. I think I was on Facebook or Tumblr at the time, and I wanted to create a username. I just put "Ugly" in front and ran with it. I didn't think of "U Gotta Love Yourself" at that time. A year or two later, I realized I wanted to start my own brand, so I decided to figure out what "Ugly" stood for because I didn't necessarily want it to be something negative. That's where "U Gotta Love Yourself" came from. It's just something I lived by, and it fit.

G On your Instagram, you posted a photo with what I perceived to be a daughter on her father's shoulders holding a Black Lives Matter sign. In the caption, you wrote that you never thought you would be experiencing any of this. Did you not imagine seeing these protests and the continual murder of black people at the hands of police, and with that, how are you processing everything that's going on?

B Not in a million years. To be honest, I was pretty ignorant to the things going on with race. Obviously, I knew black people were mistreated, and I have my own experiences, but at the same time, I was one of those people who was just used to it and accepted it. Now, with everything going on, I'm floored. I'm a little older now, so I feel like I have to do something; I have to be a part of this. Even if you are not getting cuffed up right now, it can still affect you, and it's going to affect your kids and other people's families if something isn't done. Right now, I have to figure out how to do my part, and it has got me thinking a bit more seriously. I am just trying to find my role, even if it's painting the real history of what's going on with proper representation. My goal is to get my artworks into a museum so kids of all colors can see them and say, "Yeah, I can do this too." There's plenty of stuff that can be documented from our lens rather than just a white one.

G You've spoken about being kicked out of your dad's place while living in Chicago and subsequently being homeless. Do you remember where your head was at and how you felt in that moment?

B My home life wasn't absolutely terrible; we had lights in the house and things like that, but money was tight. It's not like I had never been through anything, but at the same time, I was freaked out and nervous that first night. I wasn't thinking about any of my goals; I was just thinking about food and shelter, like, "Where am I going to stay in this big-ass world?" The world just seemed so much bigger, and I seemed that much smaller. But at the same time, I put God first and just walked in my faith. I am not bragging on myself; I am just really focused on my goals, and when I put my mind to something, I pretty much get

it done. That is one of the moments in my life I will never forget. It took everything I had in me to overcome it. Of course, I still have fun, but I have a more serious approach with things now. I try to be positive with the things I say and do. I'd rather do the action than speak on it, you know?

G You've also mentioned that at that point in your life, you were afraid of the dark and were not able to eat at times. Is that something you still struggle with, and if not, how did you get through that?

B Now, I am doing better. I didn't have an eating disorder or anything. I just wasn't making any real money at my internship, so I wasn't able to eat. I got paid like twenty dollars every two weeks, so I started selling my clothing, computers, and stuff like that. As a kid, I was always afraid of the dark. Not knowing what your future holds is kind of like the dark. I spent so many nights alone, it almost felt like I was always in pitch-blackness. I think it was a sink or swim moment, and that's how I approach life. Even if it's something as minor as cutting the grass, if I say I'm going to do it at 1 p.m., I have to keep my word. That's what motivates me.

G You're an artist creating in various mediums, be it clothing, painting or design. What's the intention with your practice, and is there something specific that you're working towards within your work?

B When it comes to the art side of things, it's not about being money hungry or greedy. I want to get my family secure and be able to help others; that's why I've become a jack of all trades. I want people to know that they don't have to box themselves in. I feel like that's what life was telling me, and I recognized at an early age that I didn't need college. I felt like it was boxing me into one career, and honestly, that's the new generation's mindset right now. We've broken down so many traditional barriers. You don't have to do just one thing. Moving forward, there are going to be a bunch of kids doing everything. You will be able to go to one person and see a bunch of different things.

G What would you tell a young person, or anyone for that matter, who's trying to love themselves but may find it hard?

B The only advice I would give is to accept your fate. Obviously, you can create your own fate, but I think loving yourself is about appreciating those moments of solitude. Everybody is completely different; no one is going to do what you do how you do it. We have some similarities, but the best part about a person is how unique they are. Overall, that is the main goal. Outside of the art, it's about getting people to feel good about themselves because that's how inspiration is sparked. I see somebody doing something, and I'm like, "Damn, I can do whatever I want to do as well." It's not like I have to make T-shirts or paint, but I can literally cut grass and start a business. Whatever it is, you have something to contribute.

EVERYBODY IS COMPLETELY DIFFERENT; NO ONE IS GOING

TO DO WHAT YOU DO

HOW YOU DO IT.

KAJAHL

Pg. 50
Alchemist, 2016
Oil on canvas
36 x 24 in
© Kajahl Benes.
Courtesy of the artist and
Richard Heller Gallery

GLENN You may be most known for your show on HBO called *Problem Areas*. In season two's mental health episode, you cover many things, but one thing that stuck out to me was the Anxiety and Depression Association of America's claim that half of all mental illness begins by the age of fourteen. What kind of teen were you, and did you have any seeds of depression, anxiety, or other issues growing up?

WYATT Yeah, at that age, you're trying to figure out who you are. I definitely felt depressed as I tried to figure out where I fit in, and I was trying to get a sense of who I thought I was and who I wanted to be.

G You also mentioned in that episode that you see a therapist. Was there ever a hesitation to meet with one? Has it helped you?

W I do see a therapist, and I've found it to be very helpful. Having someone who you can talk to about things and who isn't a friend or family member with a particular bias definitely has value to it. When I initially decided to go to a therapist, there was definitely a hesitation. There was a certain element of "Oh, you don't have anything to really complain about. Just push through," and I think that winds up being an unfortunate impediment for people to do the work that could be very helpful to them in ways they don't even realize.

G In your sophomore stand-up comedy special *Brooklyn*, you opened up about your father's murder and even dedicated the special to him. One thing that stuck out to me in your special was when you spoke about how you responded to seeing the murderer's mugshot. You stated that you didn't feel anything when you saw his face. Was there ever a sense of bitterness after your father's passing, and what was the grieving process like for you?

W There was tons of bitterness. I felt very angry and unsure, and in many ways, I wanted revenge on a person I only knew as an idea. I look back at it now, and I get it. There's a lack of control you have in that. When I think about that, I think about being a child and becoming a fan of Batman, and that came out of that connection. "Look, here's somebody who's lost and look how they've been able to come out of that and turn it into something where they've been able to get justice for themselves." You look at revenge as justice.

G Within your comedy, there are so many topics that are covered. With *Problem Areas*, you were diving deep into various issues, but in your stand-up, you might say a joke and tie it into a bigger issue, such as gentrification. When did you get to that point? Did you always see comedy as a vehicle for that, or was that something that naturally happened due to the things you saw in the community?

W I think it's a mix of both. When I look at a lot of the comedians I was influenced and inspired by, like Richard Pryor, Chris Rock, Dave Chappelle, and Wanda Sykes, they were talking about social issues. There were so many people I could see who were having these conversations, and it didn't matter how far back I went into it. When I started getting into comedy, the people I would watch were the people of the moment, but even when I looked back at comics, like Marsha Warfield and Dick Gregory, I realized so much of black comedy is connected to social issues impacting black people. I think those things went hand in hand for me. Also, in comedy or any kind of storytelling, you pull from your own experiences, so it forces you to be an observer of the world around you. It's a difficult thing to observe the world around you and not see injustice. It's nearly impossible to not see the challenges you and your community face on a daily basis.

G You've had the opportunity to work with many writers over your career. Can you share advice from any of your mentors or collaborators that has particularly affected you?

W I think one of the earliest things somebody told me was "Speak to your truth." It's very easy in a creative space to try and guess what other people may or may not like and try to cater solely to what you think the market wants. In doing so, you can lose yourself and what makes you special. You can lose what makes you and your voice unique by assimilating to what someone else's idea of good is.

IT'S A DIFFICULT THING TO OBSERVE THE WORLD AROUND YOU AND NOT SEE INJUSTICE. IT'S NEARLY IMPOSSIBLE TO NOT SEE THE <u>CHALLENGES</u> YOU AND YOUR COMMUNITY FACE ON A <u>DAILY</u> <u>BASIS.</u>

GLENN LIGON
Pg. 55
Self Portrait (VII), 1996
Silkscreen ink and gesso on canvas
48 x 40 in
Collection of San Francisco
Museum of Art SFMOMA
© Glenn Ligon.
Courtesy of the artist, Hauser
& Wirth, New York,
Regen Projects, Los Angeles,
Thomas Dane Gallery, London
and Chantal Crousel, Paris

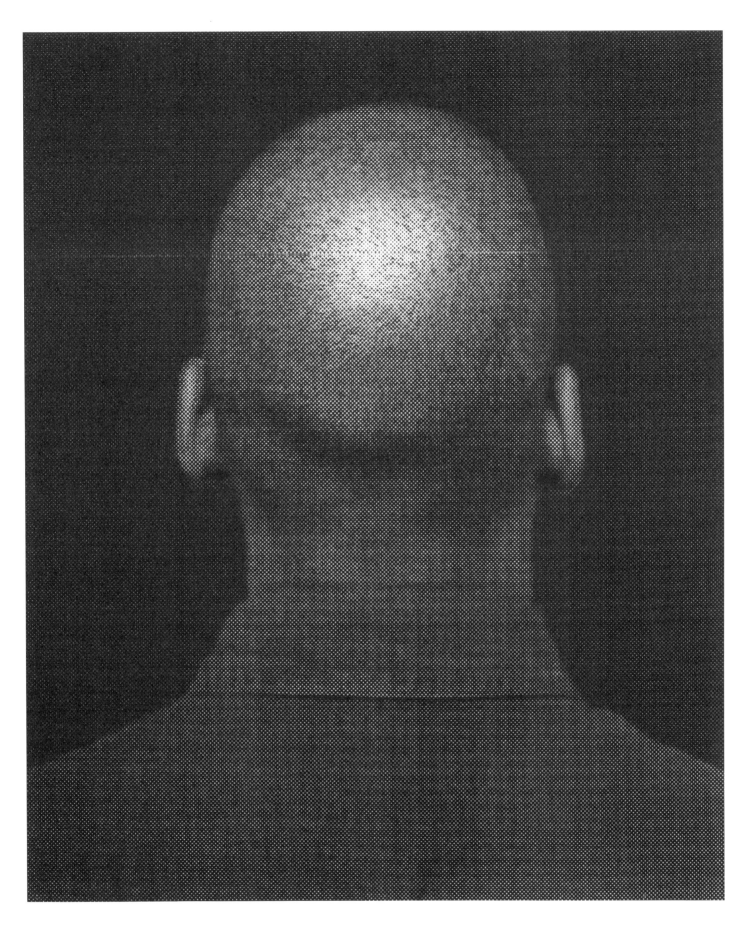

WILBERT

COO

PER

L.

GLENN You were raised outside of Cleveland, Ohio, in what you've described as "a conservative community made of second-generation white flighters." Can you speak about growing up in those neighborhoods, and did you feel "othered" at all as a kid? If so, how did that affect you?

WILBERT Yeah, definitely. I grew up in Strongsville, which is a suburb of Cleveland. One of the reasons my parents decided to move out there was to get me into a better school system. The home my parents lived in when I was born was in Cleveland Heights, which used to be a really nice suburb of Cleveland. I was going to private school in Cleveland Heights, and even when I was in private school, it wasn't as advanced as the public schools further outside of the city in the white neighborhoods. The private school I went to in Cleveland Heights was a much more integrated school. There was a mixture of black families, white families, and Jewish families.

When I moved out to Strongsville, it was all white. I was the only black person in the class, and one of maybe three black people in the entire elementary school. I was interacting with kids who had never met or played with black kids before. It was a big challenge for me, and an even bigger challenge than my parents realized. Kids will say anything; they don't have a filter. Being called a nigger or even hearing that word wasn't uncommon, so I got into a lot of fights as a young person because that was the way I responded to that negativity. Looking back, there was a lot of internalization I did in terms of being othered in that society. I internalized a lot of those ideas, and I'm still working through that now. I'd try to make white people feel more comfortable in my presence or try to show them I was smart by knowing a lot about their culture as opposed to celebrating the culture that came from my household or my community. I wanted to be validated in their eyes.

It's hard to understand racism as a kid. Looking back, I can see how conversations I had with teachers and professors over the years were colored by race. I had one teacher who was definitely a racist. She went out of her way to break me down, overregulate me, and discourage me in various ways. It wasn't until I got into other classrooms that other teachers began to tell me, "Wow, you're really good at writing." I was even placed into advanced classes. But that particular teacher gave me Fs in writing assignments. Those were the kinds of things I was dealing with, but those things are hard to understand as a kid. Why does this teacher not like me? Why don't they treat me like everyone else? Why do they automatically think I'm bad? You don't get it, and you begin to feel like it's your fault. It can take years to realize that it's not.

G You grew up with both of your parents and have opened up in multiple op-eds about both of them working in law enforcement. How did you view having police officers as parents? Was there pride or embarrassment attached to their profession for you, and did those feelings change as you got older?

W Yeah, my parents are the weirdest people, so they don't represent typical police officer parents, even the typical black police officer parents. My parents are very left, very politically minded, and into radical political thought. There was always this dichotomy between the work they did, what they would talk about, and how they would talk about things at home. My mom was one of the first black women to work for the Cleveland Police Department in a zone car. Before her, most of the black women in the police department weren't allowed to carry a gun or go on runs. My mom came into the police department after there were riots in Cleveland due to police brutality. She joined the force because she wanted to be someone who could advocate for her community. She was with the rioters; that was her perspective.

My father had more of a cynical perspective when he joined the force, coming from the ghettos of Cleveland and recognizing that a lot of his peers growing up didn't make it out. They ended up going to jail, becoming addicted to drugs, or dead. He saw it as "If I can get with the powers that be, maybe I'll have a chance to survive and have some sense of dignity and manhood in my life." They both had different reasons for joining the police force, and even though I don't necessarily agree with either of them, I understand why they made that choice coming out of the world they came from. Throughout the time I grew up, they were very critical of policing. You hear people today talking about how the police are an extension of slave catchers. That's stuff I heard growing up. My parents knew how racist cops could be because they worked among them. Their perspective was trying to make the best of a bad situation, and they would talk about trying to use what little power they had within those small interactions to support black people and not be oppressive.

I've always had respect for my parents and their perspective. It's become more complicated as I've grown older, but I understand why they made the choices they made. As someone who works in media, I understand how hard it is to be an individual who holds certain values and does certain things, while being a part of a larger system that's fucked up.

JUSTIN KEENE
Pg. 59
Liam, 2019
© Justin Keene.
Courtesy of the artist

I THINK THAT'S
THE BEST PART OF WHAT
I HAVE GOING ON NOW:
RECOGNIZING

THERE'S A PROBLEM,

GOING TO THERAPY, AND
TAKING TIME TO MEDITATE AND THINK
ABOUT HOW I CAN BE THE
BEST VERSION OF MYSELF.

SEAN BROWN

Pg. 62-63
Room For Research,
2018
© Sean Brown.
Courtesy of the artist
Photo Credit:
Mike Rousseau

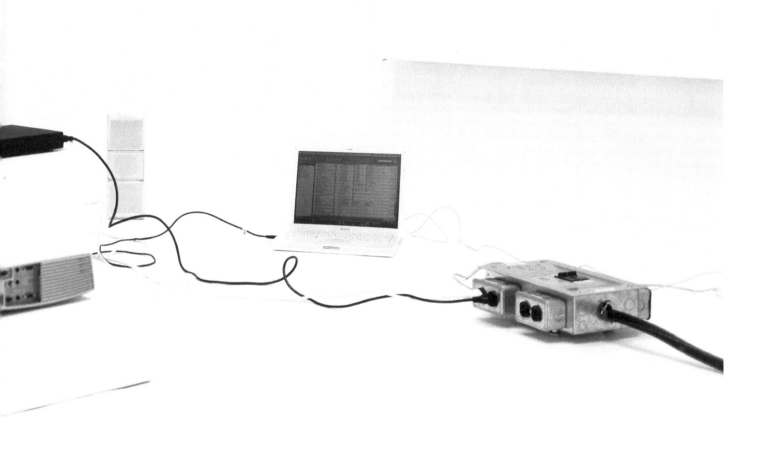

I worked for *VICE* for many years, which we know has a history with #MeToo and the representation of black people. I could go out and interact with black people and press people in a certain way, but that doesn't necessarily change how the overall company is constituted and how the media in general is constituted and exploitative. These are the challenges we face any time we're engaged in this capitalistic society.

G You've written a lot about race and masculinity in your career, and I wanted to ask you about a couple of your articles. In a piece you wrote for *VICE Magazine* titled "I Was Forced to Fight, Now I'm Learning to Cry," you write, "I'm still working my way through that maze of machismo, but instead of wallowing, I'm discovering a path out. In my early twenties, my go-to solution was to drink, numbing myself, silencing the feelings I didn't want to feel or acknowledge…" Can you speak about the time in your life when that began to change for you?

W It's still something I'm working on now. I think that's the best part of what I have going on now: recognizing there's a problem, going to therapy, and taking time to meditate and think about how I can be the best version of myself.

Drinking and finding ways to distract myself were a big part of my twenties. It went both ways. It was the partying, but it was also working. Work can be a distraction. When I worked at *VICE*, I put all of myself into work and the idea of the company, and that didn't leave a lot of space for personal growth and personal reflection.

I think, for me, race is this external thing, and it has done things to me. This "macho" thing has affected the decisions and choices I've made that have either hurt people around me or have hurt myself in pursuit of living up to a certain ideal. I'm trying to unravel that and break that down a bit so I can be the best version of myself,

treat the people in my life with love, and go into relationships and friendships with a positive and fruitful approach. The macho stuff was one of the things that held me back, and I still deal with it. It's not like it's over for me. I'm thankful that because of some of the people in my life, I've been pushed to see the problems there and continue to do the work to break that down.

G You wrote an article titled "All Masculinity Is Toxic," in which you conducted an interview with John Stoltenberg and examined his writing. What did you take from that conversation, and have your ideas of masculinity, specifically as a black man, changed in recent years?

W I think John Stoltenberg is brilliant, and I conducted that interview in a way where he could speak for himself. I know how controversial his ideas are to some people, and even when I conducted that interview in an objective way, I got tons of hate mail because people were so opposed to the ideas. I think he's much smarter than me, and part of that is probably because he's been a lot more immersed in the feminist movement. I think his ideas are very accurate and spot on, and what I take away from his ideas are that the way we define manhood in a lot of ways is through conflict. When you walk into a situation, you get your manhood by taking it from someone else. You can see that in interpersonal levels, and you can also see it on global levels, whether we're talking about colonialism or war. These relationships we have define how the world works, and that radical perspective he and a lot of women have had is important. I think John is great because he's a man talking to men. I think it's important for us to move beyond the conflict that defines our time and get to a place where we don't have to put other people down or make somebody smaller to make us feel bigger or stronger.

There's a movie I saw at the TIDE Film Festival called *Catch A Girl* by LeRon Lee. Basically, the short film is about this boy and a girl who are playing a game where the boys have to physically catch the girl and, if I'm not mistaken, kiss her. It really speaks to these ideas that we're talking about. I can remember being younger and going to the mall to see who could get the most numbers. Or you'd go to a party, and you'd try to see who got the most dances. My era was the crunk era, so you'd just go up behind a woman and start to dance with them. There wasn't a lot of consent in those settings, and that was how you defined yourself. If you were able to get what you wanted in that situation, it made you more of a man.

My big brother is a player in the old school sense of the word when it comes to his relationships with women. In that whole player thing, there's a big element of manipulation and twisting the truth to get the result you want. I was very influenced by that. Now, I can look back and say, "OK, there's something not right about this situation where you go into a relationship, and you're always trying to take, this idea that you get your identity and power from your ability to take." I want to redefine how I relate to people. So, I get that some of John Stoltenberg's stuff is radical and beyond where I'm at, but I think there needs to be more voices like that in the conversation, voices that say there isn't just toxic masculinity and good masculinity, but maybe the entire way we've constructed masculinity is not good, and we have to break it down. I'm on a journey to unlearn things I've learned and try to be a better person.

G In the article "There Is No Transcending Race in America," you open up about a hate crime, in which you were attacked outside of the *VICE* office. You were sucker-punched and called a nigger, and you've also written about similar experiences in other essays. Where was your head at in the aftermath of that attack, and were you able to let it go, or was there a deep anger or bitterness that lingered within you for a while?

W The instances of those things are really tough because when someone calls you that, it's a catch-22. On one hand, it's supposed to be the worst thing you can call somebody, so you're expected to react angrily. My parents told me, "If someone calls you that, pop 'em in the mouth." At the same time, if you reacted violently to someone calling you a racial slur, you're becoming someone who resolves their problems through violence as opposed to handling it intellectually. It's an awful position to be in and navigate as a kid. I had it happen to me as a kid multiple times, but when it happened to me in New York, it was a really sobering event. I had always recognized that Strongsville was a somewhat racist place and had always had this idea that not all white people were like the white people I had grown up around. When I came to New York, I was in this cosmopolitan, elevated sphere, and I thought I was beyond that. The night I was punched, I was with a group of very eclectic and creative people. I had some success in my career. I was making some money, living in Williamsburg, and I felt like that dude!

I thought New York was this special place, and that made me realize there was no escaping it. Now, I have a lot of black friends who grew up in New York and who've lived there their whole lives. Looking back, I think how naive I was to think that New York was this place I could move to and escape this. When I talk to my friends who grew up there, they're like, "Man, I've been getting hassled by the police since I was eleven." My idea of what New York was had privilege because of how I came here. I wasn't kicking it in Crown Heights or Flatbush; I was in Williamsburg, where things operate a little differently.

When I was punched, it turned into a bigger situation because I was with a group of people, and everyone started fighting. I decided to call the police, and when the cops showed up, the white guy who started the fight was gone. They were able to track the person down, and he spent the weekend in jail. I say that to say, there's no right way to handle this shit because you shouldn't have to deal with this shit in the first place.

DAM
DAN

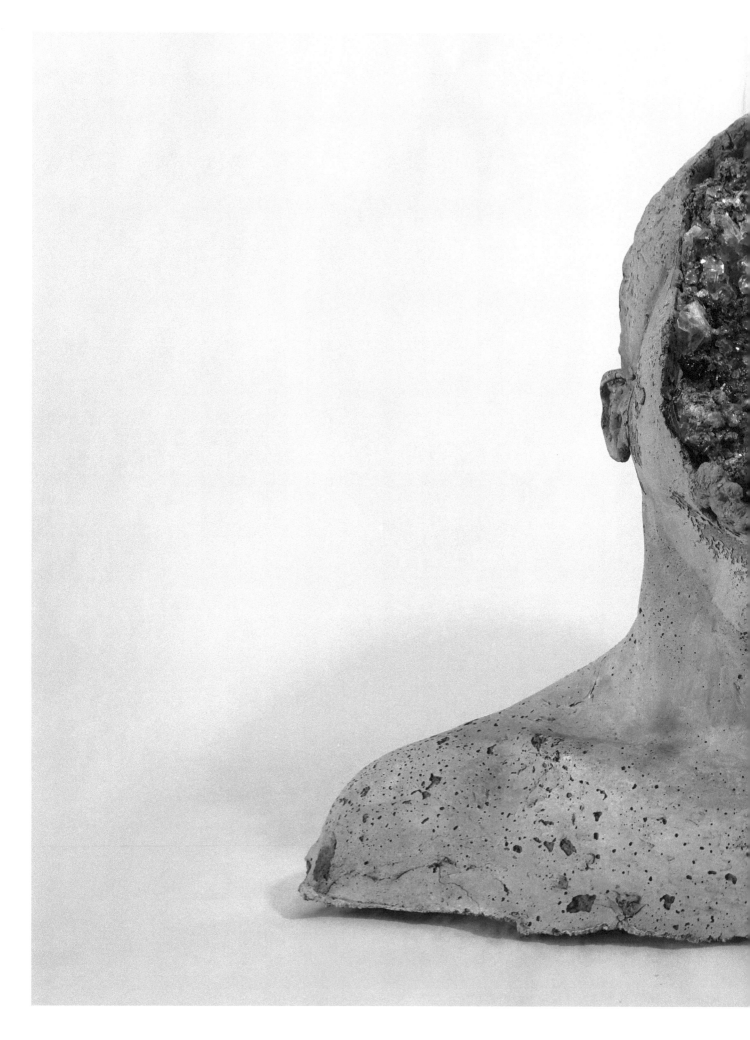

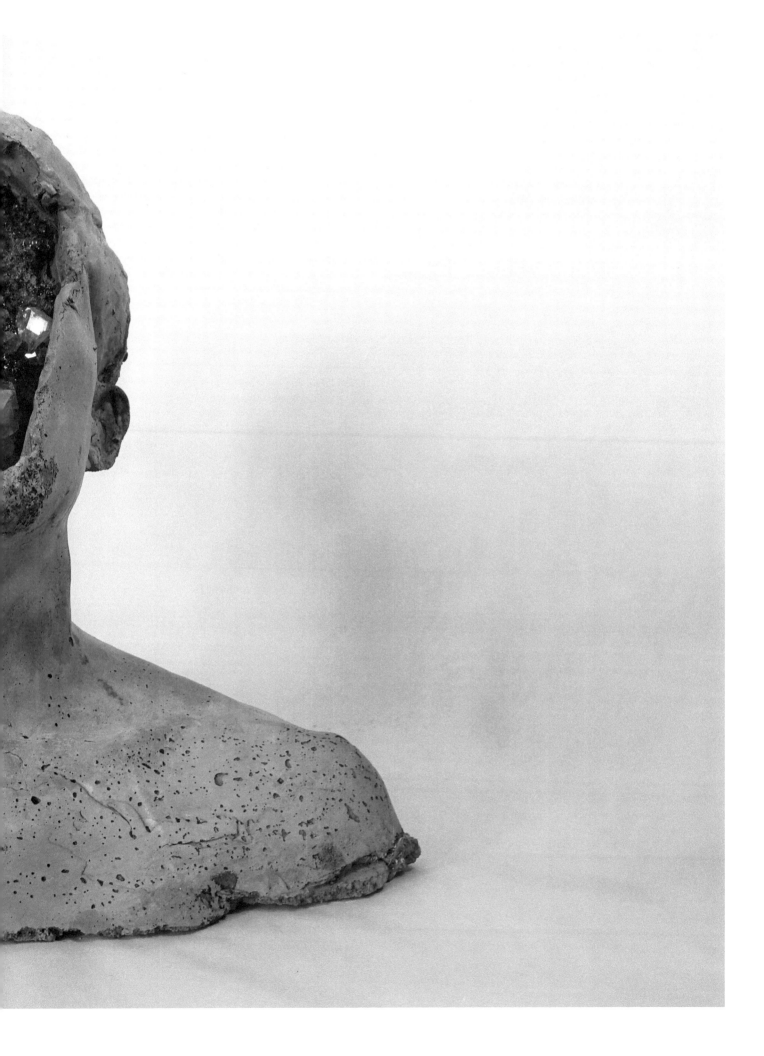

GLENN You grew up in East St. Louis, and in your short film *A Story to Tell*, you opened up about your parents being older when they had you, and that your older siblings had moved out of the house when you were a small child. I've heard you mention that you spent most of your time alone in those formative years. Can you speak about growing up in that way, and did that ever have adverse effects in your life?

DAMON Growing up in the hood and by myself, I was a nerd, so I was kind of socially awkward and wasn't the toughest nigga on the block by any means. I was an emotional artist. My brother would come home from the Army and be rough and aggressive with me. I think he was trying to show me how to fight and not take any shit because he was the oldest, so I got a lot of shit from him. My dad had fought in Vietnam, and he was an angry motherfucker, and I wasn't like him at all. I wasn't made for the Army. I had a conscience that other people did not have in my family, and early on, that was considered a weakness.

As I got older, I learned how to use my feelings in the artwork, and it helped me. Growing up, it wasn't always an asset. I knew how to befriend the tough motherfuckers, so a lot of that helped me survive because my friends were aggressive dudes, and they weren't like that with me. They were smart as fuck, so when we were hanging out, it was cool, but when problems came, I also had both of my parents who were other factors; my homies had to deal with it, and I didn't. We aligned on the things we liked, and when problems came, they could put that shit on faster than me. They were fighting in their houses on another level; their traumas were very different.

G In your TED Talk, "Courage Is Contagious," you spoke about fear in a real way, and that courage isn't found in the absence of fear but in the midst of it. You opened up about the fear around presenting on that stage, the fear you faced when SWAT appeared during peaceful protests in Ferguson, and you also mentioned fear as you experience it in day-to-day life. You even said, "I lived with fear every day. I can't remember a day when I didn't." Can you speak about the root of that fear and what that fear looks like for you?

D I think I'm just honest about what it is, and that different people call it different shit: anxiety, nervousness, numbness. We try to make up things because fear has a negative connotation in our society. Everything, all of the emotions, are either fear or love, and they grow out of that. Hate is fear or hate is love, like you could love something so much that it hurts you and turns into hate. Those aren't polar opposites in the way we try to make them out to be. When I said that, it's me coming to a realization of what I am dealing with in my own life, and I think everybody feels that. That is what I was trying to get across. I'm not different or special; I'm just real about what is going on. Also, not being afraid to kill anybody or go to prison doesn't make you tough or courageous. A lot of that is straight stupidity because fear lies within us for a specific reason.

Throughout my life, I've learned that a lot of the fear or nervousness I get is attached to me failing. I am not really afraid to die, but I am afraid of not doing what I want to do before I die. Death has always been right next to me in the neighborhood I grew up in. I grew up on a good street; I was just in the hood with a lot of older people. Death could come to you at any time by someone you know or at the hands of the police. As we get older, disease is killing motherfuckers, and the police is still on you. As I do better in my career, I become more and more aware that poverty is real. St. Louis isn't New York or Los Angeles, so it's much more difficult for people to achieve their goals. When people see you, you become a target, and there is a lot of shit that could kill my black ass. I've learned that I can't let fear cripple me, but being unaware of my surroundings and what could happen to me is the most dangerous thing I could do. Walking around in a bubble like a lot of white people do is asinine for a black man who comes from where I'm from. It is detrimental to your survival to be afraid of something. So it doesn't cripple me, but it is tangible.

Some people would say it's less fear and more of a precaution, and some people will even say you're paranoid. Yeah, I am paranoid for real reasons. I have been in real situations and don't trust people. They make paranoia sound like it is coming out of nowhere. It is a useful thing, and I think the source of it is everyday life. Some of us have different experiences. For a lot of black men, women, and trans people, shit can happen to you. When I have kids of my own, I am going to teach them that the feeling will be there for a reason, and I'll teach them how to deal with it. If it becomes something that debilitates you, you're going to have a problem. But a healthy amount of everything is there for a reason. Moderation and balance is the key to all of this shit, and you can't let it stop you from doing what you want to do, but you better listen to it when it comes up.

G You were interviewed alongside Patrisse Cullors-Brignac for *VICE Magazine* in 2018, and I wanted to ask about a comment you made about art being reactionary to the struggle. You said, "I definitely think it's an important side, much like armor. It's a defense, but also, there's only so much shit you can sustain mentally. That's why a lot of us are fucking depressed. Even right down to the rappers of this generation who are super fucking depressed. You're listening to the music, and you're hearing that art reflecting life, and it tells me that I'm not the only one in that place. A lot of black folks are in that place." Can you speak about that place for you? Would you describe it as depression, and what does that look like or what did it look like in your life?

DAMON DAVIS

Pg. 68-69
Cracks VII, 2019
© Damon Davis.
Courtesy of the artist

D I have struggled with depression for as long as I can remember, man. I don't remember ever being in a state of pure happiness. I meet a lot of people who ask why I'm not smiling or laughing or dancing. I don't think everybody exhibits happiness the same way. I think some people are searching and acting happy, like if I think a certain way, I am going to be happy. That ain't happiness! I am much more focused on contentment. It is about balance. If I'm not pissed or sad at some point, then something is wrong with me. Too much happiness is wrong too. But I don't want to get to a place that is all negative, so I have to mentally get up and work to not see things from a negative point of view.

What has helped me through the pressure ever since I was a little kid has been art. Drawing and making beats has been my therapy because I didn't grow up with any therapists in my house. I am so happy for the kids who are able to get help, but that has never been no black shit. That has always been seen as something weak people do. We have been taught to be punching bags for the rest of the world. We are supposed to work our asses off and have nothing come back to us. That is a narrative that has been perpetuated by black and white people. Black people won't even go to the doctor for their heart; we don't go to the fucking doctor for anything, then we wonder why niggas are overdosing on drugs and why crack is being used to kill, and why so many of us are dying from diabetes and cigarettes. I have tried to stop more times than I can remember, but when things get bad, I rush to get myself a cigarette and a drink because I am self-medicating. That was what I was taught to do.

One thing that didn't necessarily play out was making things; I just learned how to make that shit into a job. Now that I am older, making things is attached to a job and working; it does not do the same thing for me anymore. Now I have to go to a therapist. I love what I do, but sometimes that shit causes anxiety. Sometimes I start drawing, and I remember I should be working on something else like some pieces for a gallery or audio or notes for a film. That thing that used to help me get away from trauma has now turned into a source of anxiety. One thing that is still very pure to me is making music. I can still make beats, and I'm using a whole other part of my brain. I'm not talking; it is all emotions and feelings. Out of all the things I do professionally, writing rhymes and making music has been the least successful in the most positive way. I haven't been signed, I don't have to run to these tours, and because of that, I still find peace in it. I am much more known for film and art, so they have a different weight to them and I am trying not to let that get to me.

71

G You released the powerful documentary *Whose Streets?* with Sabaah Folayan in 2017, and the film showcases the uprising in Ferguson that took place after the murder of Michael Brown. Can you speak about creating that film? What was your intention, and when did you know you wanted to make it?

D I get that question a lot, and the more I think about it, the more I think people genuinely think everybody be out here on the come up. I was running around on the activism shit, and I was protesting, and it wasn't time to make a movie until the indictment happened. I was trying to help organize, and because I was an artist, I went to a meeting one time and I was the only one who could draw. I ended up being the nigga making the posters and flyers, and I knew what venues we could hold our meetings at. I used everything I had learned from music and other art projects as a weapon. So when it was time to make *Whose Streets?*, I was just pissed at all these outsiders talking about us like we were stupid fucking animals. People hear my accent and think I'm country, but if I had a British accent or a fucking French accent, people would think I'm smarter. But because I sound country, people thought I was dumb. That got to me because I know I am not stupid, and I know these people around me are not stupid, and there ain't nothing wrong with them because of the way they sound.

On top of that, these niggas were coming out, talking about black power this and that, yet they talked down to you. I don't need your help; I didn't ask you to come down here. I didn't ask for your help. I got to a point where I decided I had to do it myself. Somebody from the neighborhood had to do it. I was also gaining respect because I was getting locked up with niggas. They knew me because I was around, so a lot of that helped me. I'm the guy who makes shit, and I knew we had to go deeper, so I decided to get footage. I went out to shoot without a professional camera, and ran into Lucas Alvarado-Farrar who ended up being the director of photography for the movie. Then, through him, I met Sabaah, and she wanted to direct it. After talking to her and hearing where she was coming from, I believed in her, and from then on, we started working together. This ain't no *Black Panther*. Making a documentary ain't about getting rich, but I knew it was going to be a record from the people's point of view. I knew I had to do it right, and I had to do it well. I had to take the people into consideration.

I wanted to share a message from black people's point of view. I wanted it to be very micro and very St. Louis in the same way *Boyz n the Hood* was very Los Angeles. When you watched it, I wanted you to know where they were, see what they had on, hear how they talked, and feel how they felt. My goal was to uplift the beauty of the people. Whether they were men, women, gay, straight, or trans, they were all black and they all showed up to call out the oppressors. It was for the sake of putting our differences aside when the devil came to fight against us. That was the beauty in it. We still have our own shit we need to work out as a community, and I know it isn't perfect. If we can't talk to and critique each other honestly, I don't know how far we will get. Black people come into the room angry and ready to fight all of the time because we get beat up all the time. Everybody comes in ready to fight, whether it is against you or the white man. I think we need to hold each other with some grace, and I saw black people coming together with love during those protests.

G Another series I wanted to ask you about is "Negrophilia," which was a series of paintings you created that "address the intrusiveness of looking at black people dying and the effects on both the oppressor and the oppressed psyche." When you're creating a series of works like that, I imagine it can be heavy. When it comes to letting go of that weight, do you have ways of generating peace outside of the art?

D My artworks can get heavy, but art has always been the escape for me. I also watch a lot of movies, and I like to watch stupid-ass movies. Sometimes I just want to see some funny shit or watch a movie from my childhood. I like to go for walks and runs and listen to instrumentals. A lot of jazz, beats, and scores. It speaks another language around emotion and feelings where there is no dictation of how you should feel through the lyrics. I also talk with my partner because we are both into a lot of similar things that can sometimes be heavy.

I also began meditating. Recently, I have been taking a different approach to meditation so I can have a better control of my mind and fight anxiety. If I can control where my head is at, I won't have to worry about being nervous and anxious. It is like an exercise, and if I can deal with my anxiety, I'll be better off. I spend a lot of time with my sisters, my brother, and the homies I grew up with because they know me beyond *this*. I try to keep the people who care about me around and stay locked in with them. The simplest shit is what carries me through.

G Earlier, you spoke about growing up with your brother and father, who presented a certain style of black masculinity, often rooted in stoicism and violence. When did you begin to question whether you would adopt that style of being?

D Man, as far back as I can remember! I just knew I wasn't the tough guy. I would get made fun of and get in fights. I have been called everything from "white boy" to "gay" and everything in between. In high school, like you said, I was doing things that were not me, and it was obvious. I was around people who were wearing masks, and mine felt like it was always slightly off and never fit right. That is what masculinity is. Some of the masks fit, and for others, it doesn't fit that well, and I couldn't wear it the way everybody else could. Even in my life, up to twenty-five or so, I still tried to push my circle self into a square hole, trying to be these things I was told I should be. When I genuinely let that go and got mad, the aggression came from a real place, and I didn't like that feeling. I have a lot of that inside of me, specifically from the men in my life. From my real father and the abuse I took from him, verbal and not so verbal. From niggas out in the street or the societal image of black men.

I was raised by hip hop, and some of the people who made me feel human were André 3000, Kanye West, and niggas that grew up in similar conditions but didn't come out like everybody else. They weren't drug dealers or weirdos. They were completely confident in who they were, even when people pushed them to be someone different. Whenever you don't listen to those people, you get bigger and bigger and bigger. You're right, and you've always been right, and you have to constantly tell yourself that you are right when no one else does. It's going to be hard to turn yourself off to that, especially being a black man. They were my heroes, same for Jay-Z and Tupac. I know Tupac was a classically trained actor. He was raised around Black Panthers. He got all of his money after he got out of jail. Even as a child in 1996, I could see that nigga was acting, you know? That nigga was in movies, and the one who was really about that shit was Biggie. He was really quiet about it, but Biggie was the one selling dope.

There is a difference between being a singer and an artist, and Tupac was an artist. He could make you feel certain things using only his voice. I know I have that too and that I am able to empathize with others. That has always been my power. Growing up, masculinity was a problem for me. Being empathic and sensitive when many others couldn't do that was my strong suit. My daddy tried to beat that shit out of me because he was a black man who grew up in segregation. He knew how bad America could be, so that was his way of trying to help. At least, that's what I would tell myself. My brother was twenty years old when I was born, and he wanted me to be tough too. A lot of my siblings went into civil service, and I was the black sheep. I wasn't going through the Army or police academy, and I paid for it. We were broke, and sometimes the state jobs were the only ones that were available, but I just couldn't do it; it wasn't for me. I chose to pursue what I wanted and be myself unapologetically.

MY GOAL WAS TO UPLIFT THE <u>BEAUTY</u> OF THE <u>PEOPLE</u>. WHETHER THEY WERE MEN, WOMEN, GAY, STRAIGHT, OR TRANS, THEY WERE ALL BLACK AND THEY ALL SHOWED UP TO CALL OUT THE OPPRESSORS.

IONY

DEMBY

GLENN I wanted to start by asking about your mindset and vision. You're the owner and creator of Humbleriot, which uses music, culture, and storytelling to create social impact, and you've partnered with brands and organizations, including Google, Microsoft, and The Obama Foundation. One thing that sticks out to me is compassion as a core value within your company. We're in this unprecedented time, and humility in the current landscape is scarce. People are angry, and we've seen how that anger has manifested, in many ways bringing about desired results. Can you speak about advocating for change and what role you see compassion, or even humility, playing in that fight?

ANTHONY In terms of the "current time," I think we're living through two pandemics. I think about what is happening around COVID, and I think about what is happening around race. Are you referring to both of them?

G Yes, but specifically the fight for equality in this current moment.

A So for me, a couple things come to mind. My company has always focused on holding space for a number of different voices, whether that be gender, ethnicity, or background, to ensure that when we are having a conversation around anything, we are always hitting it from multiple vantage points. There's not always that kind of diversity.

People talking and listening to each other can co-create new narratives. The way the world was as we knew it is gone. I hear all this talk around when things get "back to normal." It's not going to happen. Normal is gone, and the way we're living isn't exactly for everyone. I'm focused on what the next "normal" and new reality is going to look like. I'm devoting my energy to that, and to do that, I have to think about compassion, and before I can be compassionate about someone else or my work, I have to be compassionate toward myself.

One of the benefits of COVID—and thankfully, no one in my family has gotten it so far—was that I spent a lot of time indoors alone. I have been able to clean out my mind in a lot of ways to see what was in there. The harder I am on myself, the harder I may be to other people. My main goal was to find ways I can be compassionate with myself so I can look at the world and my work more compassionately, even regarding race. I have a lot of white friends who have been calling to check in on me and see how I am doing, and understandably, they have been very timid. I've been having challenging conversations and maybe calling some people out that I really care about. In doing so, I've had to have compassion for their level of discomfort around discussing these things.

G I've heard you speak about the ego and how it aims to protect us but ultimately limits us. You've also discussed books like *A New Earth* and *The Untethered Soul*, and how many of us use race, gender, nationality, our professions, etc. to define ourselves, and how, in truth, we're so much more. In a world where our story and accomplishments are often our currency, especially within the entertainment industry, how have you understood the role of your story in your life? Also, how do you balance those aspects of your life and utilize them without being a slave to them, if you will?

A Yeah, a couple things come to mind. One, I do my best to express gratitude. I think about all the things I've done and have been allowed to do in my career, and that is a blessing alone. I remember asking my mom to pray for me about a project I wanted to get on board. She said, "Do you ever stop to say thank you for all the things you have been given?" Now, I try to stop and remember that.

When I first got into the music business, I used to write a journal entry every year. It was like my time capsule so I could look back and see where I was in my life at that time. When I first got into the music business, I knew it was cutthroat from the stories I've heard, the things I've seen and read about, and the mentors I talked to. I remember I wrote this journal entry, and I was so hungry to get into the business, but I didn't ever want to grow fangs. I didn't ever want to bite someone else to get where I wanted to be. So I always think about that, and thankfully, I was never wired that way. Sure, I'm ambitious and am striving for things to happen, but they can't happen at someone else's expense, you know?

David Brooks always talks about the resume itself, the eulogy itself, and the road to character. The resume is about titling your accomplishments, while the eulogy is for when you move on from this life. What's that thing folks say about the way you made them feel? I often think more about how the eulogy and resume can point to who I am at this point in my life. Like right now, I'm really focused on trying to learn new things and transform my fixed mindset to a growth mindset. As opposed to just moving around those mental and emotional walls, I'm looking at why those walls are there in the first place and who put them up. So, to answer your question, I do my best to stay in a state of gratitude and look at how I can reframe the bad things that have happened in my life and find opportunity within them.

JOSHUA MICHAEL ADOKURU

Pg. 81
Joshua Michael Adokuru,
Untitled (Will), 2020
© Joshua Michael Adokuru.
Courtesy of the artist

81

YOUR ATTITUDE DETERMINES YOUR <u>LATITUDE,</u>

AND FOR THE PAST COUPLE OF YEARS, I'VE BEEN BEGINNING MY DAY BY ACKNOWLEDGING THREE TO FOUR THINGS I'M <u>GRATEFUL</u> FOR.

I think about the song "Brand New" by Rhymefest and Kanye West, which has a line that says, "Your attitude determines your latitude," and for the past couple of years, I've been beginning my day by acknowledging three to four things I'm grateful for. It can be as simple as being thankful I woke up. I'm thankful I am able to go to the gym. I saw my friend last night, and they paid for dinner. The simple things that put me in a line of gratitude early in the day set the tone for what I am about to walk into. I do that every day.

G I heard you speak about being introduced to meditation by a friend, and that before you embarked on that journey, you were "at the mercy of your own anxiety." Can you speak about that time in your life? How did anxiety manifest itself before meditation?

A At the time, I was managing artists, and being a manager is a twenty-four-hour job. You always have to be on, and being in service to someone else meant I had to focus all my attention on what my clients were or were not doing. They were challenging to deal with, and I took the hard times personally. I was dealing with their stuff *and* my stuff. It got to a point where I just didn't have the tools to deal with it all.

I went with a group of friends to hike Machu Picchu, which was a life-changing trip. The day before we reached Machu Picchu, we went on this optional day hike. I later found out that this spot inspired the book *The Celestine Prophecy*. So, I ended up going to this mystical place on the hike with my friend Danielle. We walked into one of the elaborate fortress there, closed the windows, and closed our eyes to meditate together. It was my first time doing it. I remember I felt so peaceful in that moment. I felt like if my life were to end right then, I would be OK with it. I also felt like my ancestors were looking down on me. I left there feeling different; that trip changed me. I came back wanting to get actual meditation training. That was about twelve or thirteen years ago at this point.

G You grew up in a Christian household, and at this point in your life, you have a different view in terms of spirituality. What was that transitional process like for you? Do you remember when you began to be presented with new ideas?

A Yeah, I think that Peru trip got me into meditation, and when I came back, I started meeting teachers and was able to dive deeper and deeper into my practice. I began to realize how I had a connection to spirit without knowing what it was. I became more aware, and I started seeing and experiencing more. I'll be honest with you; it was uncomfortable and it scared me. I noticed how much spiritual energy was in my apartment and I started to see things in there at various times.

One of the biggest shifts for me happened when I went to see a guy called "John of God." I went there for the first time with my friend Tony, and I will never forget this as long as I live. I did a psychic surgery with him, and beforehand, they tell you to lay down for twenty-four hours after the surgery and fast—no food, no water, etc. I can't really describe the session. For a few seconds, he held my hand and spoke to me in Portuguese. They told me what he said, and I was supposed to sit down; it was that simple. But he opened me up fully, and after I left, I went back to our little hotel and got on the phone with a girl I was seeing at the time. She asked me how it was, and I couldn't really explain it, but it was pretty powerful. All of a sudden, everything electronic in our hotel room started to buzz—the phone, the A/C, the TV. I knew something was telling me to get off the phone. So I hung up, laid down, and slept for maybe eight hours.

G You've had the opportunity to meet and work with many interesting minds over your career, from The Dalai Lama to Deepak Chopra. Can you share some advice from any of your mentors or collaborators that have particularly affected you?

A A name that comes to mind is Skip Miller, the longtime manager of Lionel Richie who passed away some years back. I met Skip when I worked at the label Lionel was signed to. My boss was out of town and asked if I could take Lionel to the radio station. Of course, I agreed! I was lounging at the radio station when Skip came up to me and asked about my career goals. I told him I wanted to work in A&R (Artists & Repertoire), and we ended up talking about it for a while. Skip and I developed a friendship and he became a mentor for me. I would keep him current about the kids and what was happening in the streets, and in exchange, he would bless me with his knowledge. Sometimes I would go to his office and we would just talk. He would play me music Lionel was working on, and I would give him feedback. I would sometimes talk to him about how challenging it can be as a black man in the business, and he would always say, "Just be a man and be a good man. Focus on that."

When I first moved to NY and started my business, I moved around a lot and connected with a lot of people by putting long hours in. I remember one of my good friends Marc Gun said to me, "You know, busy is not a business model." It floored me, and I always go back to that moment when I find myself checking boxes for the hell of it. I'll say to myself, "You are not moving the needle; you're just busy right now."

MARK BRADFORD

Practice, 2003
Video (3 minutes)
© Mark Bradford.
Courtesy of the artist and Hauser & Wirth, Zurich,
Switzerland; photo by Sean Shim-Boyle (detail); courtesy
of the artist and Hauser & Wirth, Zurich, Switzerland)

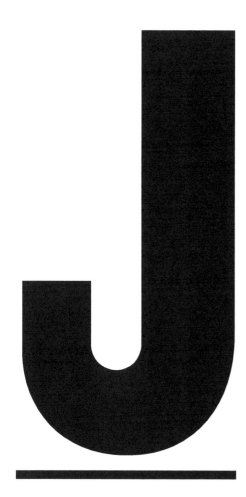

D

ARD

JAMEL SHABAZZ

Pg. 88
Black Power, 1980
© Jamel Shabazz.
Courtesy of the artist

GLENN I wanted to start by asking you about your move to California from New York. You were in film school at Syracuse University and transferred to USC, but dropped out after one semester because you couldn't afford it. Do you remember your living situation and where your head was at during that time?

JD Yeah, it was super scary. I was living at USC and had been interning at a company during the fall semester, and I basically knew when I started school in September that it would be financially difficult to come back in the spring. I was living with four roommates in a two-bedroom apartment about a block away from campus. I started to put my feelers out there and think about the fact that I would have to put in a leave of absence, which even then felt like it would be temporary. Through total luck, cosmic force, and the grace of God, someone got promoted where I was interning, and the open job had a start date of January 1. So I interviewed for that position right before Christmas break, and shortly after that, I got the call that I got the job in TV production script development.

G I read that while you were working in that position, you decided to leave and go work as a receptionist at Bad Robot. I think a lot of people stick with the gig that pays well out of fear, uncertainty, or just bills. Can you speak about that transition? What did you expect from that shift, and was there any fear in making the leap?

J Honestly, I think the two scariest pivots and pursuits of my early career were dropping out to begin with and making the jump to Bad Robot. On one hand, Bad Robot was a place I always admired. I had always been a huge fan of JJ Abrams' work and the stuff that came out of that building. But yes, if I got the job, it was going to add an hour to my commute, and I didn't have a car back in those days. I was taking the bus from Santa Monica to LA for almost two years. It was worth it, though, and being able to rub shoulders with one of my heroes was enough. Being in the type of environment to create the work I wanted to create provided enormous psychological income.

G As a director, have you ever dealt with anxiety on set?

J I have, and I think it's one of the really bizarre ironies of this work and a lot of creative fields. If someone painted a single painting, I don't think they would call themselves a painter, you know? You make a movie and suddenly you are a director. That's not to say imposter syndrome is debilitating, but it's this thing where I've *only* made two films and shot three episodes for television. The process is ongoing, and with time and experience, my confidence builds. However, I think the thrill of being able to make a film swallowed the anxiety of actually doing it.

Directing an episode of HBO's *The Outsider* really helped in terms of my growth as a director. I was desperately trying not to appear like it was my first episode. When I shot my first two indie films, I was working with talent on a slightly different tier than these actors, and I was working with a much smaller budget. To go from that to working with established actors who were fifteen to twenty years my senior brought on this new anxiety of wanting to be taken seriously. I say all that to say, my main goal was to do my damnedest not to appear so mortified during my first television experience. Truly, the only way to combat that was to be as supportive as I could. It was a wholly new experience.

G As a kid, I remember thinking the kids in films didn't look like me, whether it was *Jurassic Park*, *The Goonies*, or *E.T.* Creating films with black leads, specifically genre films, isn't that common. Did you ever have that feeling as a kid, and can you speak about what it means to you to make a horror film with a black female lead?

J I feel like my awakening came late. Part of it is because the things I was interested in, like *Star Wars*, were so great, deep, and rich. I was aware that Lando was the only person who looked like me. Part of it is because, as young black kids, our perception was that white is normal. Films didn't look any different from *Star Wars* to *Jurassic Park*, like of course the heroes are white. As I grew up, I realized that through my writing, I would be able to fight against that. When I put pen to paper, I was like, "Oh, I'm the one who determines who these characters are." It took a little bit to galvanize what my mission would become, but truly, not to be overly simplistic, I really am just trying to tell stories where those who don't normally get to do the cool things do them.

The fight for narrative equity and equality needs to be fought on many fronts, whether that is justice cinema or simply casting a black person in a role that was written for someone white. But I feel like even in that instance you should do a quick rewrite and honor that change instead of just casting someone different. I have aspirations across genres and for many types of stories. I want more promotional black heroes besides Black Panther. While that felt like such a beacon of light in this conversation, white kids have a lot more options of toys to buy. Not that it's about the hyper-commercializing of toys, but I use that to illustrate the point. It's knowing that I can go to the store and get all of these things that are for me instead of being the kid stuck in the six-inch aisle of brown toys. That part of it is really important to me.

THERE'S A NECESSARY <u>RESILIENCY</u> THAT CAN ONLY COME FROM <u>BELIEVING IN YOURSELF.</u> SOMETIMES RESILIENCY IS MORE EFFECTIVE THAN TALENT. SOMETIMES IF YOU CAN JUST BE THE LAST PERSON STANDING, <u>YOU WIN.</u> IT DOESN'T MATTER HOW GOOD YOU ARE; YOU JUST HAVE TO STICK IT <u>OUT.</u>

G While preparing for this interview, I came across a post on your Instagram page where you opened up about a nearly fatal car accident that you survived in September 2017. You wrote, "Gratitude is the paramount feeling." Do you remember some of the thoughts and feelings you had surrounding that accident? Did you come out of that with a new outlook on life or a new sense of being?

J The accident was such a crazy time and, ultimately, such a defining moment in my life. Outside of the obvious sentiments surrounding my family and my partner, after I got hit by the car, I was processing what just happened and, at the same time, slipping into a fear of death. The way I can describe it is it was this despair-filled moment where you are emotionally putting things in their mental boxes, preparing to leave. I dealt with family, said goodbye to my parents and sister, and said goodbye to my girlfriend. Then, I was left thinking, *Damn, I've only made two movies. I had really planned to do more than that.*

I think that was the first time I fully understood the idea that there will be a day our figurative IMDb pages will stop being updated, and that is what we made. There is a finite number, and we don't know what that number is. It could be two, or it could be sixty-five. Who knows? It did inspire me to like and be proud of as many things as I can on that list. It has adjusted the work I take on, not necessarily in any overt way, but I think it has become a part of my DNA and how I look at what I spend my time on. If I am ever in that position again, I would like to feel like I did my best in leaving a collection of stories that are meaningful to me and hopefully others.

G Was there ever a doubt that you would get to the place you are now as a director during that period of high school to college? Did you ever have those doubts, and did you need to overcome any internal or external voices?

J I feel like there is a degree of self-delusion you have to break through; otherwise, it is entirely demoralizing. I think in some ways you find a lot of ego in this line of work. You have to coach yourself into believing in yourself enough to survive the beginning of your career. There are so many people and circumstances that will tell you different. In my early career, the news was my archnemesis. I looked at all of the things I aspired to make one day, and there was a white male director attached to this and another white male director attached to that. At a certain point, it started to feel like an assault, and it perpetuated the idea that I'll never make it.

The trick is telling yourself you will break through. There's a necessary resiliency that can only come from believing in yourself. Sometimes resiliency is more effective than talent. Sometimes if you can just be the last person standing, you win. It doesn't matter how good you are; you just have to stick it out.

DANNY

DUN
SON

94

DANNY During quarantine, I was trying to make myself busy. I wear a lot of white shirts, usually tunics, and they have these round, mandarin collars. I've gotten these shirts from around the world, and they've become my uniform for the spring and summer. I had about twelve shirts that I had sent to the cleaners, and when I got them back, they were slightly dingy and not nearly as bright as I would've liked them to be. I could also see some perspiration marks and yellowing under the arms and around neck that didn't quite go away. I thought, *Wow, I just want them to be as white as when I bought them. I wonder if there is a way to restore them.* I started looking up online remedies and home solutions, and one website said to soak your whites in a plastic tub with baking soda and just enough water to cover them for six hours. I read another article that suggested the same thing but with a cup of vinegar as well, and another article said to add a few scoops of OxiClean powder. I didn't have any, so I just added all of my shirts to a plastic tub with water.

I looked deep in the back of my closet and found a bag I used to put things in for the cleaners. I opened it up, and there was another shirt in there that I had worn one time about four years prior. I guess I had stuck it in that bag, tossed it into my closet, and forgot about it. I took it out of the bag, and because it was tossed aside for four years, any kind of yellowing or staining had increased to a brownish color; it was awful. I was upset because it was an expensive shirt, and I didn't think it would ever be normal again, but I decided to put it in the tub as well. I let everything soak for about four hours. As everything soaked, I went on Amazon and ordered the OxiClean with next-day shipping. I figured I'd have to do the soaking process for at least two days at that point, so I soaked them for another four hours. Surprisingly, I saw a difference. There was still a little bit of dirt on them, so I continued to soak them overnight. The next day, they looked so much better! The shirt with all of the dark brown spots was really lightening up and fading, so I put it back in the water and added about three scoops of the OxiClean once it arrived. After a few hours, it was a little bit lighter, so I left it for another thirty-two hours. There wasn't much for me to do but let the cleaning solution work, so I walked away from it.

On the third day, I came back to them, and I couldn't believe how white the shirts were. Even soaking wet, I could see a difference. Then I looked at my search results again, and it said after you have soaked them, you can put them into the washing machine with warm water, a capful of dish detergent like Cascade, some OxiClean, a little bit of baking soda, and the typical Gain or Tide. So I put all of that into the washing machine, and there wasn't a single spot on any of the shirts. The dirtiest one I had tossed aside for three or four years had absolutely nothing on it. I pulled them out and didn't even put them in the dryer; I put them all on hangers and hung them on the shower rod.

The next morning, as the sun was coming up around 7 a.m., I opened my bathroom door and was met with gleaming shirts. They were so bright, I couldn't stand it. They smelled magnificent, and I couldn't find a single spot or flaw on them. I ironed them and stored them in my closet, and they looked newer than some shirts I had just recently bought. Later on, I began thinking about that whole experiment as an allegory for everything I've gone through. This slowdown during quarantine has brought a few things to the surface for me. 1) It gave me time to methodically organize my home without the need for a cleaning service. 2) I had to get creative and think of alternative ways to clean instead of using bleach or going to the cleaners. I was able to find something more natural and more effective; it just took time. This all made me think about myself and my journey.

In 2019, I was diagnosed with ADHD. It had been undiagnosed since I was about ten years old, and I had been struggling for decades, not knowing what was going on with me. I was smart IQ-wise, and because of this, people looked over the fact that I had a difficult time focusing and producing any deliverables, such as presenting a paper or passing a math test. I struggled through high school, and I barely graduated, even though I went to a special magnet school for the academically gifted. I was in advanced placement classes because that was what I had tested into, but I couldn't meet the deadlines or get organized.

This trickled into my adulthood, and I realized I couldn't focus for long periods of time, and all of this was happening as I was dealing with my sexuality as a black male in an upper middle class family with high expectations. I always felt ashamed that I couldn't put my money where my mouth was. I grew up without ever telling my parents about my struggle because at that time, there weren't any words for it.

After trying the college thing for two or three years, I began working in banking. I would get these adrenaline rushes where I could produce for a little while and just muscle through. I muscled through and muscled through and went back to school in my thirties because my dad thought it was time for me to get it done. He knew what I wanted to do, and he supported me, so he and my family agreed to pay for school if I went back. This was before any diagnosis. They just knew I was losing all hope for myself because although ADHD is a neurological dysfunction, there are other things that can form because of it, like anxiety, depression, or low self-esteem.

Long story short, I went back to school in my mid-thirties and graduated at forty years old. People think I've been in the art world for a long time, but I graduated in 2016. At the end of 2014, my father passed away, but he had seen me advance so much that I was confident he was at peace with his goal of helping me restore my sense of self. When I wanted to quit during my third year, the professorial staff at the University of Illinois in Chicago really took me under their wings. One of my professors advised me to get off of the campus and study for a while, so I studied abroad for the first time that year. After my father passed away, I went to Morocco for six months while completing my foreign language credits, and ended up graduating there.

While I was in Morocco, I won a grant to travel to Ghana for a post-grad research program. In 2017, I curated a show with a team I managed, but it completely drained me. Once again, that thing rose up within me, and it took all I had to pull that show together. By the time I got back to the United States, I was depressed and empty from that exhibition. It was about the Middle Passage, and over four hundred people, including big names like Colin Kaepernick, came to the opening. It was a big deal and made waves in major papers, like the *Boston Globe*, but I was definitely depleted when I got home. I couldn't lift a finger. I was on the sofa for about six months, just watching TV and vegging out.

A couple months after that, I got an offer to write an article on art for a major newspaper. I agreed because the deliverable wasn't due for three months, but I couldn't get myself to write anything. My focus was gone, and it scared the hell out of me. I ended up losing that opportunity, and at that moment, I realized something had been going on for a long time, and it was time to figure out what it was. I did WebMD searches, took a bunch of online quizzes, and all the results

pointed to ADHD. I went to a couple of doctors and found myself back at the university I graduated from. Their medical department had an adult testing center where I could participate in a three-month psychological evaluation to find out what was going on with me.

By the end of 2018, I had finished my testing, and in January of 2019, a week before my birthday, they called and told me I had ADHD. I was in tears but was also so happy because that diagnosis meant something could be done. They broke everything down for me over the phone, and I began to see all the ways it had impacted my life. That diagnosis changed a lot for me. It took me a while, but I sat with the diagnosis and begin taking medication and seeing a counselor. Now I'm able to produce and create work, and my focus matches my abilities. I can actually put my money where my mouth is, and I can look at the past, see my journey, and embrace the child that didn't have the words to explain what was going on. I'm able to look at life in this cyclical way, where the past is the present and the present is the past.

I can't even begin to tell you how low I felt about myself before the diagnosis. Even when I was smiling, I was struggling to push through. Where I am now is an incredible place, and I feel blessed and fortunate. I've been taking my prescribed medications, going to therapy, doing my breathing and relaxation exercises, eating a plant-based diet, and exercising, and it's all been helping a lot. With all of that, I realized my process is my process. I can't work in today's capitalistic, corporate hamster wheel to produce this and that. Sometimes people need to soak to get the best out of themselves; sometimes it takes longer than expected. There's a lot of good stuff out there, but because we're rushing and ignoring our individual needs under this homogenous idea that everyone needs to think the same and work the same, we're unable to tap in and create the level of work we're capable of.

At this point, moving at your own pace is an act of resistance against society and politics. The soaking of those shirts has become such a symbolic allegory for me. I still need to soak, and I bet you'll never see anything as bright as me once I'm done because I have confidence in myself, my talents, my capabilities, my intellect, and my spirituality. I'm grateful, and I was able to see everything in my life play out with a simple laundering of white shirts during quarantine.

MOVING AT YOUR

OWN
PACE

IS AN ACT OF RESISTANCE AGAINST SOCIETY AND POLITICS.

L

E

F

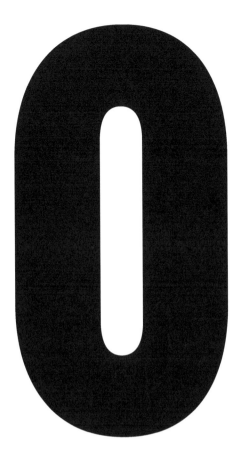

N

CARLOS MARTIEL

Pg. 100
Fundamento (Basis),
2020
New York, USA.
Performance
documentation.
Photo: Jorge Sánchez
© Carlos Martiel.
Courtesy of the artist

GLENN In your documentary short film *LEON*, your therapist diagnosed you with posttraumatic stress disorder. How have you learned to manage your PTSD? Is it through therapy, willpower, positive thinking, medication, or a mixture of all of them?

LEON Thankfully, I don't take any medication. I see my therapist every Monday, and it has changed my life. Along with therapy, I also meditate and use mindfulness as a tool to keep my balance and remain positive. In addition to that, writing has been another tool I've used to combat PTSD, and I'm very intentional about my needs. Therapy has helped me identify what those needs are and establish an environment where I can thrive.

One book I read described how our minds are like gardens. If you don't cultivate those beautiful flowers, they will fall and weeds will grow. I've become very serious about cultivating the right kind of garden, and that comes from the books I read, the meditating I do, the therapy I participate in, the music I listen to, the things I consume on social media, and the boundaries I set for myself. I keep up with current events, but I'm intentional about it and choose to not overstimulate myself. I also don't watch the police brutality videos that circulate online. I'm familiar with the cases but choose not to watch the videos. I'm very intentional about what I consume.

G Your short film *LEON* ends with a black screen and this quote: "Seeing a therapist is one of the most courageous things I've ever done in my life. I chose to heal me; you should choose to heal you." Why did that take courage for you, and when did you make the choice to go?

L I wrote about going to therapy before I even went. I wrote this piece about the different things I've experienced in my life and how going to therapy could help me cope with them. There are quite a few things I have suppressed, like my sister passing away when I was thirteen. I never went to therapy for that. After I attended the funeral, I went right back to school and didn't talk to anybody. I knew there was some deep trauma within me, and from reading books, I knew the importance of deep healing. I've talked about healing on my social media for years, but I wasn't actually doing the work. I made a decision to become intentional about healing.

OUR
MINDS ARE LIKE GARDENS.

IF YOU DON'T CULTIVATE THOSE BEAUTIFUL FLOWERS, THEY WILL FALL AND WEEDS WILL GROW.

G When I saw that word "courageous," I thought a lot about the stigma there is surrounding black men and therapy. Was there any shame in going to therapy, or did you see the potential benefits from the beginning?

L I was always open to seeing a therapist. I believe it's always courageous to choose yourself, especially in a society that applauds you for selflessness. It's become a trend on social media to be a leader. How much of that is authentic when we are suffering so much as a collective? I watched this interview with Iyanla Vanzant and Oprah, and Iyanla said, "You are the representative of God in your life. How you treat yourself is how you treat God." That interview really inspired me. I loved that I was doing great things for the community, but I wasn't happy on the inside. I had the whole neighborhood supporting me as I ran for Pittsburgh City Council, but they were supporting me in something I didn't want to do. Dropping out of that race and choosing me was tough. I was so miserable as a city councilman, but now, I'm able to live my life. I was nineteen when I got shot, so I've been a part of the system my entire adult life. At some point, I had to fight my way, not how everybody wanted me to fight.

G You've spoken publicly about the violence you witnessed growing up, including the murder of your childhood best friend and your sister. With everything you've gone through, what have you learned about processing grief?

L Grief is hard. One of the worst things to say to someone who is grieving is that it's going to get better. It never gets better; it gets easier to deal with. Every time I think of my little sister, I relive the moment she passed. Grief is the process of understanding, and it's a hard process. I'm grieving right now. My cousin passed away last Saturday from a car accident in Pittsburgh, so that began a grieving process for another person, and it builds up like layers until you become desensitized. Therapy has helped me out with that a lot. I've experienced a lot of death in my family and friend groups. The thing about the short film is that it was my first session with my therapist. I wanted to feel something because people would die, and I became numb to it. But when my cousin passed away last week, it felt so good to cry and release the sadness and confusion. It is OK to cry and be upset and angry and all of these emotions you may feel. After losing a loved one, it's justified.

I would encourage people to give themselves a safe space to grieve. We should look at death as something that's inevitable. The question is what am I going to do today, and how can I help the world? How do I want to communicate with my parents, cousins, and siblings, even if they think I am wrong? If either of us will pass away tomorrow, how will I treat them today despite all of our differences and challenges? I try to process how valuable time is and live my life bringing more joy to the world.

G On November 11th 2012, you were shot five times by the Pittsburgh police during a traffic stop. You survived, and were paralyzed due to one of the bullets striking you in the spine. In your film, you also say that "Those officers took something from me. It's not my ability to walk; it's something deeper." Have you been able to pinpoint what that thing was and is it something you can reclaim?

L It was my joy, and I think I did reclaim it through therapy. I was always smiling and happy on the outside but grappling with my internal peace. Through therapy and being intentional with my healing, I was able to get to a deeper level of understanding and find my peace. Before, I could never sit still. I was always moving, and I was a slave to my thoughts. Now, I'm able to sit still, meditate and do nothing. I'm able to enjoy me, and I've found a deeper meaning of self-love and appreciation.

G How would you define your spiritual life and meditation? Do you believe in God, or are you a spiritual person?

L I believe in God, and I am a very spiritual person. My grandfather always said, "I am a student of the living, but I practice love." I have an older brother who is a Jehovah's Witness, a cousin who is Muslim, cousins who are Christians, and aunts who are pastors. I grew up around it all, and I embrace it all. I've had Korans, I've had Bibles, I've had books about paganism, and I found inspiration wherever I could. Most religions have more in common than most people realize.

Pg. 105
Rayshard Brooks, 2020
© Yung Jake.
Courtesy of the artist

GRIEF IS HARD.
THE WORST
TO SOMEONE W
IS THAT   IT'S
BETTER.   IT
BETTER;
EASIER   TO

ONE OF THE THINGS TO SAY TO SOMEONE WHO IS GRIEVING. IT'S GOING TO GET TO GET NEVER GETS GETS IT GETS DEAL GETS WITH.

JAMMIE HOLMES
THEY'RE GOING TO KILL ME, NYC, 2020
© Jammie Holmes.
Courtesy of the artist and Library Street Collective

O KILL ME.

R.

MES

HARRISON

KHALIF TAHIR THOMPSON

Pg. 112
Blackbird, 2019
© Khalif Tahir Thompson.
Courtesy of the artist

GLENN You're a licensed clinical social worker and the CEO of Courageous Collective Healing, where you also serve as a psychotherapist. One thing that jumped out to me was the Henry Grayson quote on your website that reads, "As long as we think the thoughts we have always thought with the frequency with which we have thought them, and as unconsciously, our lives and our relationships can never consistently improve, for we will be imprisoned in the ego mind's way of thinking." Can you speak about how you address the ego with your patients, especially those who may not be privy to that language? And how has that way of thinking informed your approach with therapy?

JAMES That's a great question. I think that quote refers to how we often get caught up in our ways of being. It can be helpful to challenge ourselves, but sometimes our ego gets in the way. This is exactly what Henry Grayson speaks about in a book called *Mindful Loving*. He wrote about developing deeper connections with ourselves, and he uses the term "ego" a bit differently than some other psychoanalysts. Essentially, Grayson uses it as a means for us to understand how we as individuals think about ourselves and others, and that there's a spectrum to how that understanding is shaped. I think a lot of us come to understand that we can be influenced by our environment and our circumstances, so part of it is being able to look at how we interact socially in our environment, how we interact with our workspaces, and how we interact with our families. It can be important to step back and ask where those thoughts originated, who implanted us with that particular way of thinking, and if the way we're operating is the healthiest way possible.

As a trained social worker, we focus on biological, psychological, social, and spiritual domains and how we function healthily in each. How do we function in a biological manner? Am I aware of the things that are being introduced in my body to sustain it? Is there anything coming into my body that is going to deteriorate it or have an unhealthy impact? That kind of approach can also be applied toward the psychological, how we think and the things we are taking into our minds that can be helpful or unhelpful. Socially, are we hanging out with folks who are going to be positive and help us spiritually along a path, folks who believe in spirit and incorporate it into their lifestyles? There needs to be balance when assessing if everything is functioning in the best way possible. This is very much an independent path for a person. What works for me is not necessarily going to work for you, so we wanted to engage in dialogue regularly to ask these healthy questions.

G You've also worked as a music educator in the past. Do you think there is a link between music and mental well-being, and does music make its way into your practice somehow?

J There is definitely a rhythm that is consistent in our lives and in the practice of what I do. A metaphor I use with patients talks about the energy of rhythm and what that means in real life, using a mixture of music terminology. How do we know we are in harmony with other people? Are we able to communicate with them in a way that is not dissonant, and if there is conflict, are we able to find a resolution? Is there someone who is more dominant in the relationship or someone who is more passive? What is it like for us to engage with one another?

If something has a high frequency, it vibrates faster. We could use this language to talk about anxiety and other manifestations of high energy and movement. If someone is behaving erratically or moving really quickly, we want to find ways to slow that down for them. That can help decrease some of the anxiety that's often present in music or movement. There are various approaches for body scanning or progressive muscle relaxation. Both of these work to slow us down, focus our attention, and bring awareness to what it feels like to be inside of our bodies. All of that is related to and connected to vibration. If we create tension in our bodies by frowning, the tension will still exist if we relax, but we will experience a form of relaxation. We get to pay attention to and understand what feels good and what doesn't. If we put our hands on a hot stove, we are probably going to pull our hands away really quickly. That quick moment cultivates energy. We get to decide if we keep our hands there and let them burn or if we figure out ways to still enjoy the heat from a distance, thereby creating a healthy boundary for ourselves. You can still be a part of the environment without having to get hurt in the process.

G You were a part of the Stand Up & Knock Out Racism event in Oakland, which brought out the youth in the community to unpack biases and address how these issues are impacting them. Can you speak about that event and how you approached those topics in that setting?

J I was invited to Stand Up & Knock Out Racism by professional boxer Dalia "La Pantera" Gomez. She coordinated that event to encourage some dialogue and movement between black and brown youth in Oakland. The Bay Area is like one big family, and we were able to invite practitioners, writers, and poets to come speak to the youth about their experiences with racism, how they cope, and what actions they're taking to address the issue. We were able to uplift those who felt disempowered to make change.

The youth has a completely different perspective on the matter. Many youth are very conscious of the impact racism has, seeing people belittle, berate, and express rage toward them for being black and brown. Systemic oppression creates barriers for every age group, so it was important we have those conversations with activists, leaders, and healers to talk about what actionable things we can do in general and in specific situations. Many people spoke about how it affects their families, what it is like to deal with stress, and how they respond to tension when it is present.

When we feel we are being oppressed, how do we respond? What are our options? I want to encourage people, and we have encouraged many, to find someone to talk to in the community who has some of the same knowledge base to support their process.

When it comes to racism specifically, there have definitely been some hate crimes in Oakland. There have been a number of instances where nooses are hung around the lake or racial slurs are spray-painted on billboards. It requires compassion to go back and create art from that, to go in and inject love into these experiences for the good of the community. We can reclaim what belongs to us and take a stand. Young people can engage in art and learn about historical systems to educate themselves in a way that doesn't involve going to blows with someone or physically fighting them.

Part of Gomez's approach for teaching self-defense involves protecting the mind and going back to biological, psychological, and spiritual approaches. So the framework tries to answer the following questions: When we are not in fight or flight mode all of the time, how do we go about taking the steps to heal ourselves? What does it mean to truly take care of and heal ourselves? A lot of that involves self-care, being around folks who want to be connected in a compassionate, understanding, and loving way, and maintaining spaces that cultivate those things specifically.

G You've also hosted "Men Striving for Mental Wellness," where black men open up about the struggles, journeys, and healing that's taken place in their lives. It's a beautiful thing to see these kinds of events hosted by black men for black men, especially because in the past, there didn't seem to be a focus on our mental well-being in this way. You've been in this field for over twenty years. Can you speak about the changes you've seen, not only in regards to events like this, but in the culture and within your patients?

J I am forty-one now. Twenty years ago, I was very much immersed in the music and dance community. I had actually connected with a licensed psychiatrist and a clinical psychologist and social worker in my travels. I had gone down to Cuba, was studying music and dance there, and met two black women in the field. They said they needed more mental health help by men specifically, and they requested I come in because only a third of the practitioners looked like us and there needed to be more healing spaces for us. At that time, I hadn't really been connected with a ton of practitioners outside of these two women.

I did an internship at UCSF (University of San Fransisco), and that was a primarily white space with some clients of color, but the main focus was healing for white men. Then, I transitioned to deaf and hard of hearing folks in D.C. That was also a mixed space, but I ended up working with some youth in Maryland and D.C., where the focus was on their mental health. But on some levels, the systems and modes of sharing information were based on a medical model rather than a culturally specific approach.

When I was young, I was exposed to folks like Na'im Akbar and Dr. Amos N. Wilson. I remember going to an African-American bookstore in Chicago, seeking out some of those books, and flooding myself with the knowledge between the pages. Once I got into academia, a lot of that stuff wasn't talked about. They didn't talk about the black experience, what was happening to us generationally, and what was happening to us in the western, European system. If you wanted to get involved in anything African-American focused, you had to seek it out and run toward it. Myself, my brothers, and many other people began creating spaces for black men outside of the spaces I was already participating in. Still, they were few and far between. For example, I remember that during my time in grad school, there were more organizations built for black men to socialize than there were for mental health. There were very little opportunities for growth. If we wanted those spaces, we had to create them ourselves.

THERE ARE STILL FOLKS WHO RESIST OR HESITATE TO ENGAGE IN <u>DIALOGUE</u> AROUND MENTAL HEALTH BECAUSE THERE IS STILL A STIGMA WITHIN OUR COMMUNITIES. IT'S OK TO SAY YOU NEED <u>HELP</u> <u>WORKING</u> THROUGH SOME OF THE <u>SYMPTOMS</u> YOU ARE EXPERIENCING WITHOUT LABELING IT AS DEPRESSION OR TRAUMA.

VIRGIL ABLOH

Pg. 117
A Team With No Sport,
2012
From *Youth Always Wins*
© Virgil Abloh.
Courtesy of the artist

What I am noticing now with COVID and everything happening in 2020 is there have been more resources and services funneled toward internet-based activities. More folks are putting themselves out there to be seen, and they are becoming more aware with the technology that is available. Don't get me wrong, I think there are still folks who resist or hesitate to engage in dialogue around mental health because there is still a stigma within our communities. It's OK to say you need help working through some of the symptoms you are experiencing without labeling it as depression or trauma. We simply want to be able to have conversations around this. Not everything has to be labeled. What's important is that we have conversations and find ways to help support each other. We can say, "Yes, I have anxiety or experience depression," but that is not your identity; that is not who you are. You are not your trauma. You are not bipolar disorder. You can address your symptoms and talk about them if it has a positive effect on your greater health and well-being. It all comes down to how we think about ourselves and talk about ourselves to other people.

G How has your work affected you and impacted your life? Have you experienced anxiety to the point where you thought it might be a benefit to attend therapy?

J As a practitioner, I definitely participate in therapy. I think it's very important for practitioners to stay balanced. We do a lot of work in supporting others, and I have definitely had my experiences with anxiety, depressive symptoms, and trauma that I've been able to heal from. I think it is important for us to explore and examine our lives and what it means to even have a traumatic experience. Trauma doesn't mean you had to have been in a war or some extraneous experience. There are what we call "microtraumas" or "microaggressions" that can contribute as well, and there's definitely a spectrum for what trauma can look like.

I have a history of seeking out healing individuals, like my grandmother and music teachers, who didn't provide formal therapy but helped me seek out solutions to reduce my stress. Music, dance, and exercise help to alleviate tension and balance me out. There is a such thing as healthy stress, so it's important to look up how stress comes into our lives and how it affects us. So, yes, I absolutely participate in therapy. I have a great therapist who's a woman of color, and I definitely appreciate the perspectives she brings to my experiences, whether it is some of the professional things I am working with or the personal things. I also participate in groups with other practitioners to ensure the work I am engaged in is ethical and relevant to my patients.

G Your brother is also in the field and has his doctorate in clinical psychology. Was there a substantial focus on mental health in your household growing up, and can you speak a little about your childhood and what brought you into the field?

J My brother and I grew up in separate households. My mom and dad split when I was pretty young, then they remarried. My brother and I had a fair amount of contact coming up, and we come from a family of healers. We have a number of folks in the health and healing profession, including nurses, an uncle who is an MD, and a set of aunts and uncles who support a group of homes in Arizona. While there wasn't necessarily a focus on mental health, there was a focus on healing. Because my grandmother was a nurse, she would often create care packages; it was like a deluxe first aid kit. She made sure we had all the gauze, Band-Aids, scissors, and whatever else we needed to take care of a person's physical ailments. The mental health piece wasn't something that was intently focused on, so my brother and I are the only ones focused specifically on mental health. He's finishing up his PhD and is actually going to be coming out to California to do his post-doc next month, which we are both really excited about because we haven't been in the same city for many years. He and I have definitely had some great conversations around what has been happening in our family because, like any family, there are going to be some issues and conflicts, but also great experiences of love and appreciation. Each family loves in their own way.

That makes me think about Gary Chapman's five love languages. Each family's love languages are different. Some family members can vibe with them and some can't. You are going to find, develop, and cultivate love in the way it speaks to you. So growing up in my family, there were not a lot of conversations about mental health. We both grew up in the church, and even though my spiritual god has shifted (I am focused on more African traditions), there is still a focus on healing and prayer to establish a connection with a higher power and spirit, which was always present growing up. During my childhood, I was told we could pray about our mental anxieties, and that has very much been the rhythm of our healing. I've been able to consistently be aware of what is present for me, what has been on my mind, and what destination I want to arrive to. What is the state of being I want to embody and manifest? If I am constantly focused on the things I do not want, then I will never know what I actually want. So if I say I want to have a more loving relationship, then I have to assess myself and ask what a loving relationship looks like to me and how I should talk about it to the people I am engaged with. If I say I don't want that, then the conversation will focus too much around negativity. We want to focus less on what is not needed and more on what is needed to cultivate all the things we desire.

AJOR

JACKSON

GLENN Many of your early works looked at your hometown of Philadelphia, painting a vivid picture and drawing the reader in. You've continued that practice with your "Urban Renewal" series, often detailing conditions of dilapidated buildings and the beauty of the inhabitants. Within those poems, there's a positive vision. Does the state of today's world bring you down, and how do you maneuver through those negative emotions?

MAJOR There is an accumulated joy—I'll call it "ancestral joy",—that billions of black lives have within them to sustain emotional and mental well-being. Is there a range of emotions, including disappointment and frustration? No doubt. All of that is present. I'll never forget my grandmother noticed a certain kind of melancholy that creeps up on us. Well, for me, I guess it has been there for a long time, but she recognized a certain type of melancholy, and she was a very Christian, optimistic, positive woman. People wanted to be in her company, and she said to me very casually, "It takes more muscles in your face to frown than it does to smile. You'll look older if you keep that visage." We also kept a dictionary in the house, so anytime I heard a word I didn't know, I had to go look it up. I went and looked up the word "visage." So yes, I guess I am affected by these moments, as well as the moments that don't make the headlines.

Our friend Claudia Rankine brought attention to the microaggressions we face daily. I just wrote an email this morning in response to a colleague who was apologizing for whatever indignities I faced these past few weeks because I made it kind of public with my think piece. I wanted her to know that when we find ourselves doing this kind of work or contemplating these kinds of issues, it's not new, and for me, the method has been to focus insidiously on making this a humane, thoughtful, and safe space for all of us. I also stressed the importance of keeping our sense of joy and lightness. Whenever I am in the company of my mentor and friend Sonia Sanchez, we do more laughing than anything else. There is a certain dignity in being able to laugh during the storm.

I appreciate the substance of that question because it is self-conscious. It is a way of being versus forcing. I have a dear friend who is facing some economic challenges and is also sensitive to people's struggles around the globe, as she is a Jewish-American and has realized what she has inherited from her family. She is debilitated by this moment, and in those moments, not all of us have the same sense of joy and resilience. We have to take care of each other. I think community has been a huge part of survival for me.

G There's an essay by Gregory Pardlo titled "About Major Jackson," where he talks about your work and friendship. One thing he shared in it was a conversation you'd had where you discussed your time working as the curator of literary arts at the Painted Bride Art Center. You told him, "This was where I found myself as a writer and an artist." Can you speak a bit about that time in your life and what made it special?

M The Painted Bride Art Center, at the time, was a multi-racial art center run by artists themselves. The sense of solidarity we had was owed to the enthusiasm we had around each other's practice. We held each other up and acquainted each other with opportunities instead of hoarding growth. We were also brought together by shared interests, both political and social, that were geared toward change. We realized early on that the arts could help facilitate a difficult conversation. It was an affirming community for me to be a part of. I imagine these are the kinds of spaces previous Renaissance generations were into.

I was just reading a transcription of a conversation between James Baldwin, Alvin Ailey, Albert Murray, and Romare Bearden for a documentary about Bearden. They talked about being in Paris post-WWII in the early '50s and how being around each other contributed to their growth. You're cheating yourself if you are not a part of some kind of conversation, whether it's within a community or simply with a friend.

G While I was preparing for this interview, I read that you live in Rochester, Vermont, in the Green Mountain National Forest. Can you speak about living there and what nature means to you?

I CANNOT HELP BUT
UNDERSTAND THE WORLD
THROUGH A

SACRED LENS.

WHETHER THAT SACREDNESS
IS DUE TO A HIGHER POWER OR BEING
IS NOT MY MAIN FOCUS; I AM
MORE INTERESTED IN HOW IT HAS
MANIFESTED IN US.

M That is a great question, Glenn. My earliest years were spent in the South during the summer, particularly Tennessee and Kentucky. This was prior to the growth both places experienced. My great-aunt had a chicken coop in the backyard, a peach tree, and a rural life. My love for the natural world was cultivated between the ages of two and twelve. We eventually stopped going down there and spent our summers at home in Philly. It wasn't until coming to Vermont for the writer's conference that I realized I needed this. This scenery was so important to my writing and thinking because to be in nature is to contemplate life. Everything around you is alive. It may be foreign, but we don't necessarily need to fear it; we just need to be cautious.

Living and writing in Vermont has done so much for my inner growth. Lately, I've wanted to know the name of everything I encounter, and in acquiring those names, language has become an ongoing thirst, and I've sparked a curiosity for the world around me. I feel like I am being taught and shown the mysteries of existence. On the flip side, I have taught at NYU for thirteen years now. I can get my hair cut in Brooklyn, go to museums and meet up with friends in cafes. As much as I love nature, I also need the vibrancy of the city because that is part of my experience as well. I feel like I am understanding the privilege I have to access more or less of the city's vibrancy and opt for the quiet, measured spaces of the natural world.

G Do you have a meditation or prayer practice? If so, how long have you been doing it, and how has it changed your life?

M Yes. I cannot help but understand the world through a sacred lens. Whether that sacredness is due to a higher power or being is not my main focus; I am more interested in how it has manifested in us. Sentient beings who are relative to the Earth have an enormous amount of power to impact another's life. I would say first and foremost what I have learned is that it starts with us being attentive to our breathing and how we are taking up space in the room, the community, and in our families. From '97 to '99, a very transformative experience took place while I was studying in Oregon. Soon after, I realized all life is sacred. But coming to Vermont in 2002, three years later, was when I started to realize I needed to incorporate breathing into my daily process. It is not every day, of course, but there is a meditation app I use. Sometimes my wife and I go into a room in our home and meditate, either together or alone. I feel like if I have a particularly heavy workday of Zooms or writing deadlines, I will either start or end my day with a quiet moment. I find it helps me engage more with others and directs more of my attention.

OSBORNE MACHARIA
Pg. 127
Nywelw Za Kale #2, 2014
© Osborne Macharia.
Courtesy of the artist
and K63.Studio

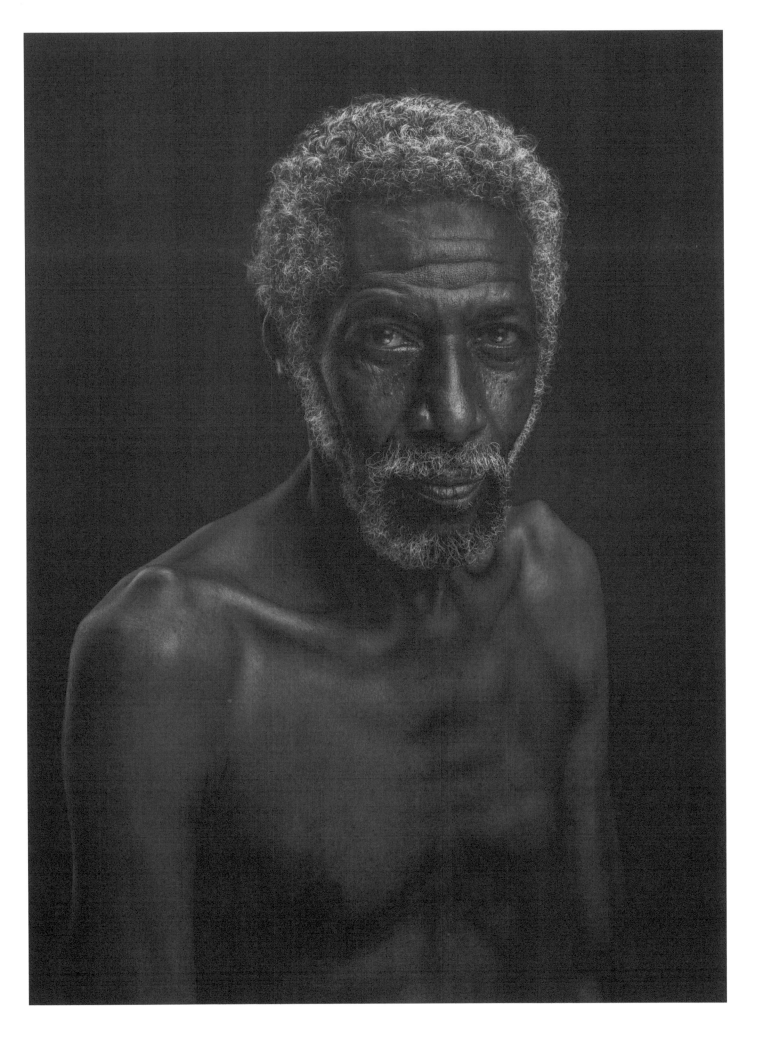

XAV
JERN

GLENN You've spoken publicly about growing up a in two-parent household until you were nine, and that during those years, your stepfather was great with you and your brother, but he was abusive to your mother to the point where she'd often barricade herself in your room. You've also spoken about meeting your biological father only a couple of times and that he passed during your sophomore year in high school. During that time, especially as a teenager, how did you make sense of what was going on? How did those stressors affect how you thought of yourself and how you moved through the world?

XAVIER For a long time, I wouldn't talk with my friends about the details of my family dynamic and my biological father. When I went to Florida A&M University, it was the first time I met a bunch of black people who came from two-parent homes. I realized I was in a minority coming from a single-parent home, which was exactly what I needed to know. I needed to know that there was this other experience because back home, there was only one friend of ours who had parents that were still together. At FAMU, my friends would say, "Hey, you don't really talk about your dad." I didn't realize it was so glaring. I would briefly explain and say, "Oh, yeah, they split up." It took me a really long time before I came to terms with my background.

In the last ten years or so, I saw my late stepdad, who I hadn't seen in a long time. He had moved out of state when I was in college, so I didn't have the chance to see him before he left. We had a nice time together during Christmas, and I saw him a few more times after that. It was interesting because I showed him pictures of my travels on my laptop, and the wallpaper picture was one of my favorites: a picture of me and him from when I was in first grade. When he saw it, he just stared at it. The love he had in his eyes took me back to those days when it would just be me and him spending time together. He loved me like I was his own.

I met my biological father when I was about six or seven years old. I remember standing there, seeing this tall, slim man and feeling indifferent. I remember thinking to myself, "Huh, OK, so this guy is my biological father." The very next thought I had was, "I already have a dad who loves me, so I'm good." That's how I felt about it in that moment and for my entire life. In the past five years or so, it became important for me to fully embrace all of me and be my full authentic self, no matter what. My brother and I don't use the term "half-brothers" because we had always lived in the same house. We are brothers; that's it. My mother had two sons back-to-back at ages eighteen and nineteen by two different guys. I didn't want people to look at my mom crazy because she had two baby fathers thirteen months a part, so I wouldn't talk about that detail.

BENJI REID
Pg. 131
Untied, 2019
© Benji Reid.
Courtesy of the artist and October Gallery, London

In my mind, I was protecting her, but I realized as an adult many years later that there must've been a part of me that thought it was a little crazy. I was projecting that onto people and not giving them the chance to form their own opinion. Once I had that realization, I was able to embrace my story fully because there's nothing wrong with our family dynamic. My mom is an amazing women and she did what she had to do to raise us. My mother actually had ovarian cancer when she was young, and she had to have her uterus removed so she couldn't have kids in her early twenties. If she had waited to have kids, my brother and I wouldn't be here. I truly believe everything happens for a reason. I believe God birthed a unique purpose for each of us to live out. My story is my story, and I have to love and embrace all of it.

The second time I ran into my biological father, my best friend Kenny and I were walking to the corner store to get some snacks. A lot of crack dealers hung around this store, but we were used to it. As we walked around the corner, my biological dad was standing there, clearly drunk, high, or both. I still remember his face to this day. He stood there with a guy who was in a similar state, and yelled, "Hey! Heeeey!" Kenny and I kept walking, but I decided to stop. He introduced me to the guy he was standing with and said, "This is my son." I remember being so offended, and thinking, *You are literally a stranger to me; I don't know you.* I honestly didn't resent him in any way for not being in my life, but I did not appreciate him trying to claim me as his son. I knew biologically it was a fact, but he wasn't my dad; he didn't know anything about me. As Kenny and I walked away, he asked me who he was, and I said, "Nobody." I didn't tell him he was my actual father in that moment, and we told each other everything. I've told him since then, but that was how I dealt with it in that moment.

When my biological dad died during my sophomore year of high school, my mom insisted I go to the funeral, but I didn't want to go. I was completely indifferent about it. It was like telling me a stranger had died and now I have to go to their funeral. I don't want to sound callous or insensitive, but it's truthfully how I felt. She insisted that I go, so I ended up going. I remember sitting there, not feeling anything except annoyance. I remember they listed my name among his children and family members and that they spelled my name wrong. I had people coming up to me like, "Oh, this is one of his sons." I wasn't rude to anyone, but on the inside, I was fuming. I knew I had to be OK with my origin story so I could fully love myself and who I am.

G I'd like to jump forward a little bit and ask about the time in your life where you left a great job and moved from Cincinnati to New York to attend NYU (New York University) and earn an MBA (Master of Business Administration) in music business. You graduated as valedictorian, which is a huge accomplishment, especially at a school like NYU. Can you speak about that day-to-day process while you were earning your MBA? Did getting good grades come easy for you, and how much studying was required to do as well as you did?

X I had an MBA and a bachelor's of science in business administration from FAMU, and I decided to go to NYU for my second master's, which was a master in arts and music business. School always came easy for me, and generally, I can memorize things and understand concepts fairly easily. Because of that, I had a pattern that started back in seventh grade, where I would start the year off with straight As, then start slacking off as the year continued. I would go to class, but I would do homework and study for tests last minute. It became a challenge to see how little work I could do and still get an A or high B. I would see my grades dip a bit, then I would do a bit more work and end up with straight As. Doing that meant that instead of graduating high school with a 4.0, it was more like 3.5.

I continued that pattern early on while at FAMU. In the beginning, I slacked off a bit, but once I got into my grad classes, I got straight As. I graduated from FAMU magna cum laude, but had I applied myself, it could have been summa. Even with the SATs, I rolled in there cold without any preparation. Miraculously, I passed several of them and had advanced credit out of history and English. When I attended NYU, it would be my last go-around, in a program I'm super excited about, which would be taking me into the next phase of my career. I would also be paying for this one hundred percent out of pocket.

I was in the same program as one of my best friends, and he graduated with a 4.0. We did group projects together and were on the debate team together, and I remember people saying, "These are some of the smartest people I have ever met and they chose to go to FAMU." I had letters from every school imaginable: Harvard, Princeton, you name it. FAMU was my choice. I knew I was going to go to an HBCU (Historically black colleges and universities) school. I am the product of an HBCU family, and my brother went to Howard. I chose FAMU over Howard because of their five-year program. So my friend and I were in this program together, and once we were in year four, he was gunning for that score; it was a goal. I remember I would say to people, "Yeah, I could get a 4.0, but eh, I just don't want to." Then, finally, it hit me one day. I said to myself, *You know, the difference between you and him is he is actually doing it.*

I remember I went back to school and said to myself, *I don't want to just know how good my good is, I need to know how good my great is.* That required me to do everything I was supposed to do. I knew I needed to read the material before class so I could discuss the material, especially in grad school. I read every book referenced, even if it wasn't required. After class, I would discuss the readings with the professor, sometimes debating with him. At that point, the tests weren't a big deal because I knew the material and understood it innately. It made it easy, and I finally realized that if I truly put my all into something, there was no limit to what I could accomplish. I needed to know that. I was never late, I always sat at the front of the class, I was always engaged, and I always did my homework on time.

I would set a schedule each day, something I picked up from the professional working world. What really worked for me was having a break from school because most of us spend our entire lives in school. You graduate high school and go off to college, then graduate from college and head to grad school. Now that I had worked for two-and-a-half years at a corporate environment, I could approach it like a job. I had time during the day to set a strict schedule for myself because most of my classes were in the evening. I would read uninterrupted for a few hours, then I would review my notes from class for a few hours. Then, I would work on my papers and homework for a while, then I would check my emails and go online to read different articles and listen to music. That was my schedule Monday through Friday the entire time I was at NYU.

Being told I was valedictorian was really gratifying. It turned out my good was pretty special, and it is OK for me to know that; I just have to put the work in. You can't lean on talent or potential alone. My greatest fear is unrealized potential. I never want my story to be, "Man, I thought X was going to be this, or he could have been that." That can't be me.

G You've had a noteworthy career and have worked at record labels including Def Jam, Sony, Universal Motown and Bad Boy. What was it like working alongside Diddy, and were there any lessons in particular that you learned from watching him run Bad Boy that have stuck with you?

X It is amazing how things all come together. The internship with Bad Boy was my first one. It was during my first semester with NYU. I was checking my NYU email, and one of the black students sent out an email saying there was an internship at a well-known label record and to email back if we were interested. I was checking my email when the email came in, so I replied as fast as I could, trusting it was something good. He emailed me back and said it was Bad Boy, and I was like, "Oh, that's dope!" I got an interview, began interning with the head of marketing, Tracy Waples, and quickly had to humble myself. They didn't care about me. I was the intern, and this was my first experience in the music industry. I was answering phones, making calls, making copies, getting food, and running to pay parking meters and move cars. Really what it came down to was the experience Puff had as an intern coming up in the game. He wanted to see that hunger in his interns. You had to do what he did while interning for Andre Harrell if you wanted to work at Bad Boy.

I got that right away. These folks did not care that I had a master's degree and was working on my second one. They were like, "Hey, if you want to intern here, this is what interns do." You had to be proactive. Say I had to make copies of a video treatment. I would make the number of copies they needed plus an extra. I would always make a copy for myself, and I read everything that came across Tracy's desk. That evolved into her inviting me to her office and asking me my opinion on things. In the beginning, when people would go into her office, she would shut the door and they would have their conversation. But as time went on, she started leaving the door open, and I could listen in. Then, it turned into her inviting me in to silently listen, and afterward, she would ask for my opinion. I told her I'd caught on to her test, and she said she absolutely did it on purpose. She said she knew I was different from the way I carried myself. She could tell I took it seriously so she decided to invite me in.

I began offering ideas about what we could do marketing-wise, and a lot of this was in the early social media space. I did some live chats with Carl Thomas and 8-Ball, and artists hadn't done that. We just started doing some new and different things, and word started going around that the artists liked working with me. One day, Diddy was hosting one of his company town halls where he would address label matters. In business school at FAMU, I learned how to form intriguing questions for the different business leaders that would come in and address the student body. Normally, certain people were assigned to formulate and ask questions, and there was a vetting process that graded the question's formulation. You would raise your hand, and if you got called, you would stand and ask the question in front of an auditorium of business students. I took that same training and applied it to that town hall because if I was going to have Diddy's attention, I wanted to ask a question that no one else would ask due to fear.

A lot of the staff feared him because he is a celebrity and carries himself a specific way. Some of the rumors are true, like the ones about it being cutthroat or coming into work and finding out someone got fired. You just have to move with a certain level of boldness, and for me, once I am in the room, if I have a question or a perspective to offer, I am going to ask that question or offer that perspective. One thing about doing that, though, is people are either going to agree and appreciate you for articulating yourself, or you will offer something no one else has thought of. Either way you look at it, it is a no-lose situation. That was my approach. Diddy began to take notice of me, and Tracy also spoke highly about me, so when I wanted to interview him for my thesis at NYU, I asked Tracy. I knew he knew me in passing and knew my face, but I felt like if I asked her, she could help me get time with him, and she came through.

As the story goes, I interviewed him backstage, and at the time, he was doing *A Raisin in the Sun* with Phylicia Rashad and Audra McDonald, who both won Tonys from their roles. It was very surreal. We were in his dressing room, and they were putting makeup on him, and as he was getting ready, I was just sitting there asking questions. He was really generous and very transparent with his answers, and we had a good rapport. He asked me what I was going to do when I graduated, and at the time, everybody knew I was going to be valedictorian. It had spread around the office, and people were excited about it. The previous summer I had interned there, I had been voted employee of the month, which never happens for interns. There was a bit of mystique around me as an intern, like "Who is this guy? Wait, he has a master's degree and is going to NYU to get another one. Oh, *and* he is going to be valedictorian? Who is this guy?"

So Diddy asked me what I was doing after graduation, and I said, with no hesitation, "Hopefully, working for you." I meant at Bad Boy, not for him directly, as Tracy was going to hire me as a product manager on her team. "OK, OK," he said. "Something close to me is opening up. I want you to go for it." I didn't know what he was talking about, but I said OK.

After I interviewed Diddy for my thesis, I headed into the office and everybody told me that the head of HR was looking for me. I mean, five different people came up to me and told me, so I was a little shook. I was wondering if I was about to get fired! I started thinking about what I said during the interview and if I offended him. On the way to the HR office, I had made up my mind that he didn't like what I said and I was about to get fired. So I started rationalizing, like *That's OK; I will just get another job.* As soon as I get to the office, the head of HR tells me to close the door. I was, like "Oh, man!" So I close the door as slowly as possible and sit down. She tells me that Puff has been looking for a protégé, someone he feels he can teach the business to up close and personal and eventually pass the company onto. At the time, it didn't register to me that she was talking about me because I had already decided I was going to get fired. I was just sitting there, like *Oh, that is an interesting preamble to letting me go on my last day.* Finally, she said, "Diddy thinks that person is you." I was like, "Oh!" She said he wanted me to work for him as his personal assistant and protégé and he was going to teach me the business firsthand then groom me to eventually take over. She asked if I was interested, and in my head, I'm like *Hell yeah!* But because I had work experience and an MBA, I knew to ask questions. Overall, though, I knew the answer was going to be yes. I started in that position a few days after I gave my valedictorian speech at NYU.

It was a tough gig. It was seven days a week, and my day started when he woke up in the morning and ended when he went to bed at night. I was with him everywhere. As an assistant, my job was to be an extension of him. I got to see and do a lot that summer. It was an election year, so I got to be a big part of the popular Vote or Die campaign he was doing. We were at the Democratic National Convention that summer, where President Obama gave that amazing speech. I got to be a liaison for everybody that came to see him after he finished a performance for *A Raisin in the Sun.* It was breaking all of these records on Broadway, so everybody came. Johnny Cochran, Hillary Clinton, Chris Rock; you name them, they were there. I was the person they talked to while they waited to see him. I got to meet so many people, and it really normalized and humanized them and those kinds of experiences. It just made me realize that I could talk to them like I would anyone else.

Funny story: Puff wanted Hillary to do something for his campaign. So he was on the phone with her, and she says to him, "What does Xavier think about this? Does he think I should do this?" He put the phone down and was like, "What in the world did you say to her? She is asking about you." Then I said, "Tell her I think she should do it." I was able to establish a rapport with people, and they all saw something in me and connected with me, and I was just being myself. Seeing them and interacting with them is simply a human experience, but being a kid from Daytona Beach makes it so unique. At three years old, God told me I was going to be in New York City one day. I literally grew up one thousand miles south of NYC, and now, here I am, waking up Puff in the morning every day, with Hillary Clinton asking for my opinion. It was a reminder that there is nothing out of reach for God.

I walk boldly in God's promises every day and try to find out how good my great is. I believe in maximizing my time on this earth and living with purpose.

Working alongside Diddy every day was a roller coaster ride, but I quickly learned a lot about how to establish my boundaries and my place in the business. Ultimately, I quit that job at the end of the summer. That was the first job I quit without having another one lined up. I ended back up at Bad Boy doing digital marketing, so it is all love there, but at that time in my life, the pace of that role wasn't good for my well-being, so I had to step away. It truly felt like the opportunity of a lifetime, and in a lot of ways, it was. I learned a lot about myself that summer.

G You also serve on the board of the Hip Hop Culture Council at The Kennedy Center in Washington D.C. alongside LL Cool J, Questlove, Common, Q-Tip, Robert Glasper, and many others. I bring that up because hip hop has been such a pillar in your life and career. You even gave a sermon titled "Hip Hop, Don't Stop" at Emmanuel Baptist Church in Brooklyn, New York. As we know, hip hop is historically explicit, and often the themes or lyrics to the greatest records can't be quoted during Sunday service. As a Christian, how have you come to understand your relationship with hip hop, an art form that, at times, may not share the same values as you?

I AM HIP HOP, BUT I DON'T HAVE TO BE ABOUT WHAT THEY'RE RAPPING ABOUT IF I DON'T AGREE WITH IT.

138

MARCUS MADDOX

Pg. 138
Awaken, my friend,
2018
© Marcus Maddox.
Courtesy of the artist
and Red Arrow Gallery

X I love that question. For me, hip hop can be appreciated on a number of levels. I can appreciate the culture of hip hop from the standpoint that it is a truly American art form and that it is a truly black, Latino, and brown art form that we created from nothing. We made something out of nothing, and it has literally moved the world. Growing up, I knew it was for me, that it was speaking to me. So I can appreciate it for the passion, the aesthetic, the graffiti, the slang, the way we talk, the way we move, and of course, the DJ and the actual four elements of hip hop. There's a beauty to the art form and putting together these lyrics that rhyme. I can appreciate the way the artist delivers their rhymes, how the lyrics come together, how the sounds blend, the style production, and the way the beat hits my ear. I can appreciate the song, even if they are not talking about something I believe in, strictly based on the way the words connect and how the sound hits my ear. I can appreciate it on that level, but it does go to another level when they are talking about something I can relate to and that reflects more of who I am. There are some things I won't listen to because I just can't do it. There are some things that are not for me, but if someone else likes it, then cool because I'm not about censorship. I just know I won't seek it out.

I have always been a purist anyway, so I'm more in the pursuit of lyricism. I can also listen to a record and not let it become a part of me. I'm somebody who has never been drunk or high, but it hasn't stopped me from going to parties or dancing and hanging out at a bar with my friends. I let them do their thing and I do mine.

I can listen to a song where Biggie is kicking in a door and robbing people, but I am not about to start kicking in doors and robbing people. I live about three or four blocks from where he lived. I've always loved Biggie, and I was really drawn to how he put words together. I love Mobb Deep and the darkness of their production and lyrics. I like to work out to Griselda Records, and can appreciate different hip hop on different levels. Sometimes something might not be the most lyrical, but I like the style of production they are using and how they sound over the beat.

My first sermon ever had to be about hip hop. It is rooted in me, but again, if I don't agree with something, I don't do it. I don't call women bitches or hoes, and if I am trying to recite lyrics I will try to omit those parts. I am hip hop, but I don't have to be about what they are talking about if I don't agree with it. I focus on celebrating the culture, and I love that it is a wholly American art form that was created by black and Latino people.

Ultimately, I believe that is why God put me here: to help people and make a relationship with Christ relatable. You can be who you are and still love Jesus. You can love the music you love and still love Christ.

G The last thing I'd like to ask you about is God. You're outspoken about your faith and how it has informed your life. How have you come to understand who or what God is?

X I remember my mom had a picture that said, "God is love." I reflected on that for years and tried to understand the notion that God is love, and it just hit me one day. "God is love." To love people as yourself, to hold God as the standard above all of us, that is what I love about God being first in my life. God is a standard above all of us, and it is a standard we can aspire to and manifest in our everyday lives. We all know to treat others by the Golden Rule (treat others the way you want to be treated), but it's more than that, and I see people as God sees them, unleashing that kind of love into the world.

I don't think the English language has the right words to describe God. The words Him and His don't cover it because those leave out women. God is all of us. I don't think of God as a man. I really believe that all of us carry a part of God, and we all are a bit of the manifestation of God. That is why it is important to get outside and look at the sky, sit by the water, and feel the breeze on your skin. Let the sun in, see the rain, and appreciate nature because all of that is a manifestation of God. I do my best to surround myself with it all as much as possible. As I get older, I understand how much more complex God is.

I'm glad I learned in high school that I have a tendency to slack off, and I use that now to work harder. I believe a lot of us are not living life in full abundance. We think this is as good as it gets, but God is trying to tell you there is so much more out there. I strive to walk in fullness and live more abundantly. That is where I am trying to be.

RL

JONES

GLENN I read that in your teens and early twenties, you were going through a bit of a rough patch, getting kicked out of different schools to even getting shot at. Can you speak about where your head was at during that time, and what your vision or dreams were when you made the choice to move to Los Angeles?

CARL I was in a crappy place because like you said, I was kicked out of school. Looking back, I don't think I was a real troubled kid or anything out of the ordinary; I was just a huge class clown. Once I started reading different books about government conspiracies and African history, I started caring less and less about school. Before I moved to LA, I started removing myself from the system, began to think about what my purpose was outside of getting an education, getting a job, paying bills, buying a house, and dying. There was something more, of course, and there was a bigger purpose.

I hustled and sold everything you can think of to put food on the table. Shortly after I dropped out of school, I had a family. I had kids and a wife, and there was a lot at stake. I was in this place of desperation before I moved to California. I was tired of bootlegging movies and watches. I had people working for me, and multiple barbershops and beauty salons selling my shit, and ended up having some bad shit happen with that.

One time, I was in North Carolina selling stuff outside of this gas station right outside the projects. Around two or three in the morning, the clubs would let out and my man would have money out there. I had a little set-up, a table and TV so you could see the movie. People get nervous about the movie having someone walking in front of it; I'm sure you remember. One time, this guy I sold *Flubber* to in front of the projects came back and told me he wanted his money back because there were people laughing in the back-ground and shadows walking across the screen. I told him, "Well, when you go to a movie theater, people laugh and walk in front of the screen, right? You can't get your money back." I thought that was clever, but he didn't. He came back with a bunch of other guys in a car and pulled out a gun. Right before he pulled out the gun, I got the vibe and grabbed my shit. He pulled the gun out and shot the glass of my van's window. My friend was ready to fight, but I was out of there. I remember coming home and reflecting on that whole scenario and what I was doing. At the time, the police were cracking down on bootlegging, and I had people coming to my door asking questions. It was crazy.

Mind you, I'm coming home late at night, drawing and writing. I would create these characters and ideas for shows. I had a big box of drawings, stacks of sketchbooks. It was something I was passionate about. I knew that was what I wanted to do with my life; I just had no idea how to get there. So I actually ran into a friend of mine from college at a Barnes and Noble, and he was telling me how he just came back from art school and was doing a comic book with an animator friend. He invited me to that guy's apartment, and we hit it off and became really close. Eventually, the animator friend got an opportunity in New York to work with Roc-A-Fella for The Play Pen project. He asked if I wanted to work on it, so I jumped on it and started designing some characters and putting a package together. We sent it off, and they loved it. They wanted us in New York, and I dropped everything to take the train from North Carolina.

When I was working on The Play Pen, I stayed at the State Property house, and I remember seeing Uzis, clips, and Percocets on the table. It was crazy, and I would be there, trying to work on the cartoons. When Beanie Sigel got arrested for attempted murder, it killed the cartoon, all puns intended. One of the producers on that project moved to LA, reached out, and told me to head to LA. At that point, I just went back to North Carolina, and I was thinking, *Damn, that was my shot*. I went back, and it was just a dead-end situation. My wife at the time literally put in a thirty-day notice on our house. Then, she told me fifteen days later that we were moving to LA. I was apprehensive, but she kept saying I couldn't accomplish what I wanted in North Carolina, so we just took a leap of faith with no plan.

G Multiple times in your career, big opportunities have presented themselves after running into someone on the street or in a store. Do you believe in luck or chance, and is it something you think is a component of your life?

C I don't necessarily see it as luck. I believe our thoughts are magnetic. I think the brain knows what we are focused on, so if we put energy into what we desire, we can draw it into our reality. When I left high school, I gravitated toward an Islamic organization that taught us about spirituality, the mind, how to manifest things into reality, and how to take control of the things in our lives. So from a very early age, I started practicing these meditation exercises and was very particular about what I wanted.

143

JUSTIN MIKHAIL SOLOMON

Pg. 144
Silhouette #4, 2019
© Justin Mikhail
Solomon.
Courtesy of the artist

At one point, I remember telling my wife at the time that I knew I was going to work on a hit black animated show. I couldn't explain how it was going to happen or when, but I could see it. It was just one of those things where everything started to align. So I think there are things that are destined, but I also think we create those things by thinking positively about the future. I believe wholeheartedly that these things came together because I was so focused on them.

As a kid, I would go through the comics in the Sunday paper, cut out all the strips I liked, then put them in one of my mother's photo albums. I did this every week until we ran out of photo albums because drawing and animation was something I wanted to do. I was always really obsessed with cartooning and comics. I was so focused; there was nothing else that existed to me. It was that important.

G You executive produced *The Boondocks* for three seasons, and amidst the comedy, there was commentary on black culture and America as a whole, which led to a lot of controversy. With that said, you've been vocal about your conviction as a writer to shake people up and spark dialogue in the name of freedom of expression and healing. Did those negative voices ever weigh on you? Was there any stress or anxiety with the backlash?

C I would say most of the stress came from the actual production itself, not so much the content. It was more about our really tight schedules. We had so many characters with so many backgrounds and locations. The stories went into some really crazy places, whereas sitcoms normally just stick to the house and maybe one other location. We would introduce new characters in almost every episode, so the scale of the show was almost at feature production level every week. Trying to fit a square into a triangle, it was nearly impossible. We would go over budget, and we would work around the clock. We would start in the morning and maybe finish around three or four the next morning. We would get a little bit of rest, then we'd be back at it. It was a lifestyle more than a job, and people's lives began to suffer, namely their personal relationships and social life. The people I worked with *were* my social life. We became a really tight-knit family.

Also, there were some team members who had children and weren't able to spend time with them. The industry is demanding, and animation is even more demanding in my opinion because it is a long production schedule versus when you are doing a short film for six months. With *The Boondocks*, it took about two years to complete a season. You go a long time without spending quality time with the people you love, and it really starts to weigh on you. That was definitely the most stressful aspect of the show.

G You opened up in an interview with *The FADER* about anxiety and how public speaking or being in front of people has led to nervousness. So many of us deal with anxiety, and it can be paralyzing, even a dream killer. Can you speak about how it manifests in your life and how you've moved through it?

C I'm still struggling with it. I was struggling with it this morning! It's a tough thing because I had to learn more about it to truly make sense of it. Not understanding it adds another level of anxiety to the mix. When it hits you, you don't know why it hit you, and you're waiting for it to stop. What I've learned is there are a lot of different triggers. For me, though, I never thought of myself as someone who was stressed, dealt with stress, or was managing stress. I didn't really understand what stress was.

I think a lot of black people have that same inability to identify stress because we have to be so tough. We have such a high tolerance for pain that a lot of it goes unnoticed. J. Cole grew up in the same area as me, and he's talked about what it was like growing up there. I experienced a lot of my friends getting locked up during my teen years. That was the time crack came out, and it literally turned the neighborhood upside down. I feel like that may have contributed to some of my uneasiness—posttraumatic stress—but I never thought about it.

Now that I recognize it, I try to control my breathing. It always hits me the worst during a pitch meeting or Zoom call. In my mind, everyone can see it, but they can't—at least that's what I tell myself. It happens to me all the time, so I try to ride it out like a storm. Sometimes I have to get away, so I'll go into a room, get under the covers, listen to a guided meditation or some music, breathe, let it pass, then I'm back to normal.

G In addition to *The Boondocks* and *The Last O.G.*, you produced the show *Black Dynamite*. That character is an alpha male, with pure testosterone, a big ego, and a hot temper. I think in a lot of ways, that's how many of us as black men were raised, and it resulted in a lot of black men bottling up trauma and depression in the name of manhood. That often leads to anger, which can manifest into violence or drugs and alcohol abuse. Have you subscribed to that presentation of masculinity, and if so, has it ever stunted your personal growth? Do you think it's an issue?

C I will speak to the character first. To me, I just wanted to make sure we were telling stories around a hero during a time where there was a lack of heroes in our community. The police aren't there to protect us; they are there to patrol us, so Black Dynamite, the character, was the hero for our community. He spoke with his fist, but it was always warranted. If he was angry with his own people, it was because they were poisoning the community or doing something else terrible. There was a dichotomy with this character as well. I've always loved characters who were walking contradictions. I don't believe people are all good or all bad, so I always like to create characters with real motivations and humanity. No matter how evil the villain, I want you to understand how their insanity came from a real place.

Even with Black Dynamite's anger and how he handles situations, if you give the proper context, the audience will be informed of where it all stems from. Sometimes the angry black drug dealer in TV or films is poisoning the community for no reason. For example, you simply see Luke selling drugs in *American Gangster*. They didn't take the time to explore what his life was like as a kid, that he experienced his relatives get their heads blown off by the KKK. As a black child, growing up in North Carolina and seeing these kinds of things happen has definitely had an effect on me.

They have the potential to influence who you become and can build some calluses on your community and worldview. So it was important for me to create context for the community itself.

In *Black Dynamite*, the community and world was the antagonist, so you got to see where his mentality came from. At one point in time when I was younger, I had a bit of a temper. I think a lot of it came from not being able to put my life into any real perspective. I didn't quite understand why my father wasn't there, why we were poor, and I didn't understand what was going on in my neighborhood. It was really confusing, and there wasn't really anyone there to explain any of it. I saw people fighting, losing their lives, friends getting thrown off of bridges, people getting shot; I mean, it was bad. So there was a little bit of anger, and I didn't know who or what to take it out on. At some point, I started educating myself, and my brothers started sharing their knowledge with me. I began to put the pieces together of why people behaved the way they did and why we had drugs in our community. Once I was able to figure out that there was a plan laid out, it all started to make sense to me.

Looking back, I was trying to find a way to escape because I didn't want to sell dope. All the niggas that had money and the latest shoes and cars were selling drugs, even the young guys. It seemed like I had to do the same thing to create any economics. I came to realize there were people who made money drawing, so that became my focus. My mother was working two jobs at once, trying to hold the family down by herself. There were a couple of times she was robbed at gunpoint at her job. I even remember seeing her on the bed counting pennies for the light bill. All of those things drove me to figure a way out of that shit. People were always telling me I could draw better than anybody else, so I was like, "Wow, I have something I can do differently than others to make some serious money." I didn't know how I was going to make it happen, but I was going to get it done. I never gave up on that dream.

STEVE MCQUEEN

Pg. 148-149
Bear, 1993
16mm black-and-white film, transferred to video, no sound
10 minutes 35 seconds, continuous projection
© Steve McQueen. Courtesy of the artist, Thomas Dane Gallery and Marian Goodman Gallery

I BELIEVE OUR THOUGHTS ARE MAGNETIC. I THINK THE BRAIN KNOWS WHAT WE ARE <u>FOCUSED</u> <u>ON</u>, SO IF WE PUT ENERGY INTO WHAT WE DESIRE, WE CAN DRAW IT INTO OUR <u>REALITY.</u>

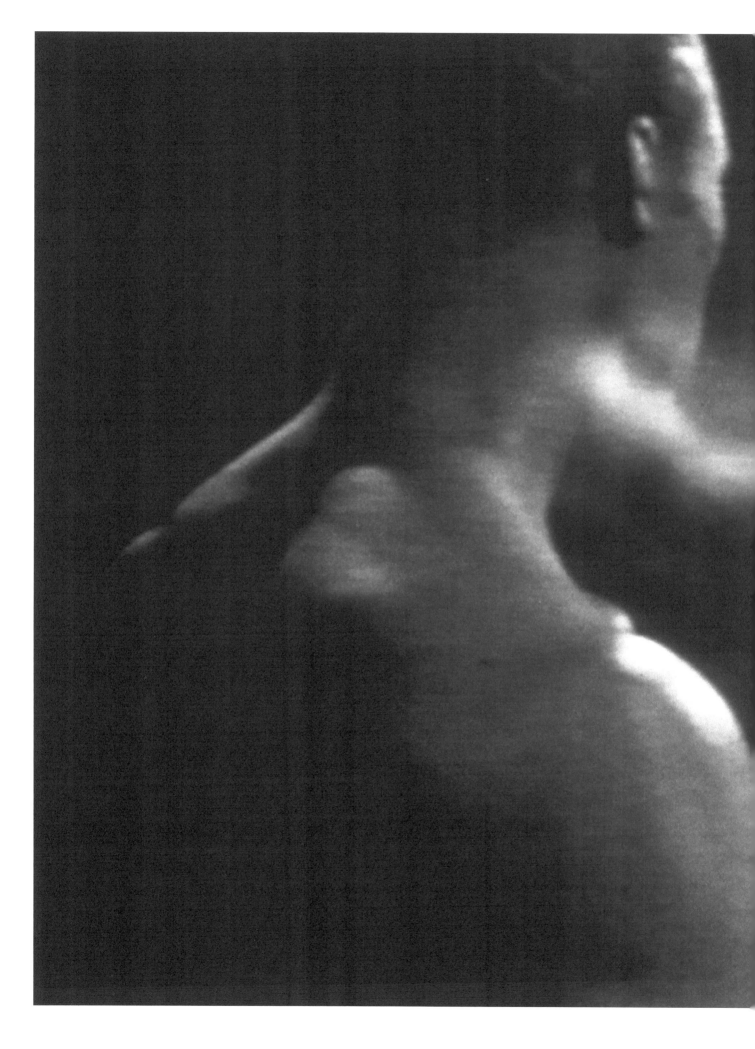

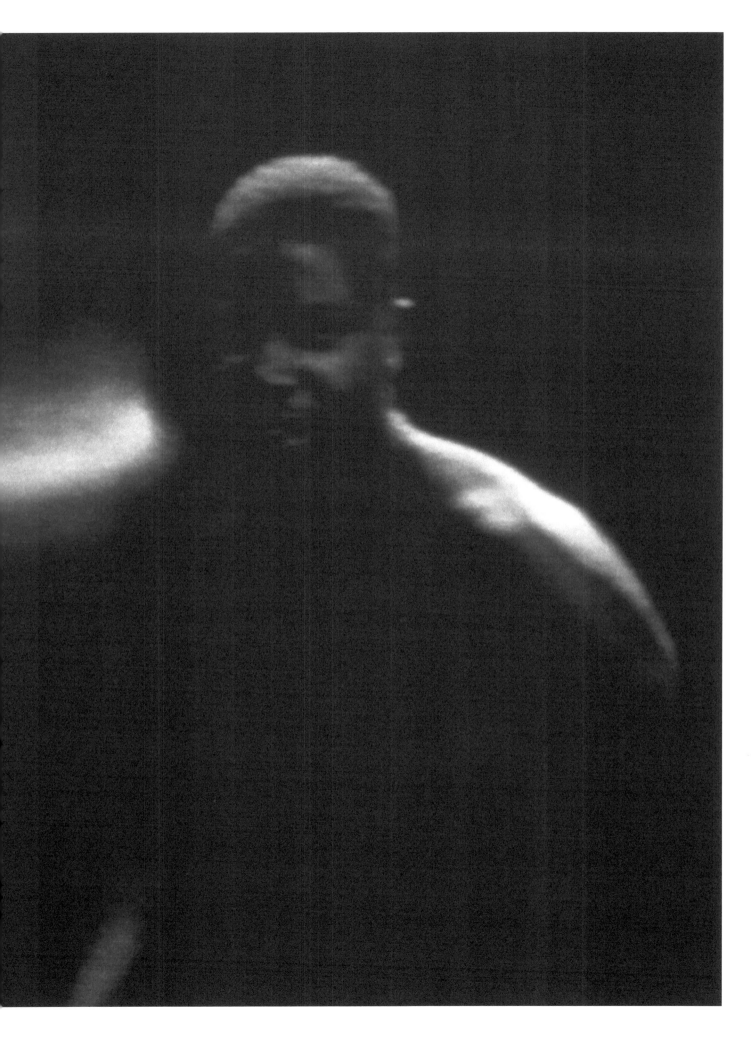

YASHUA

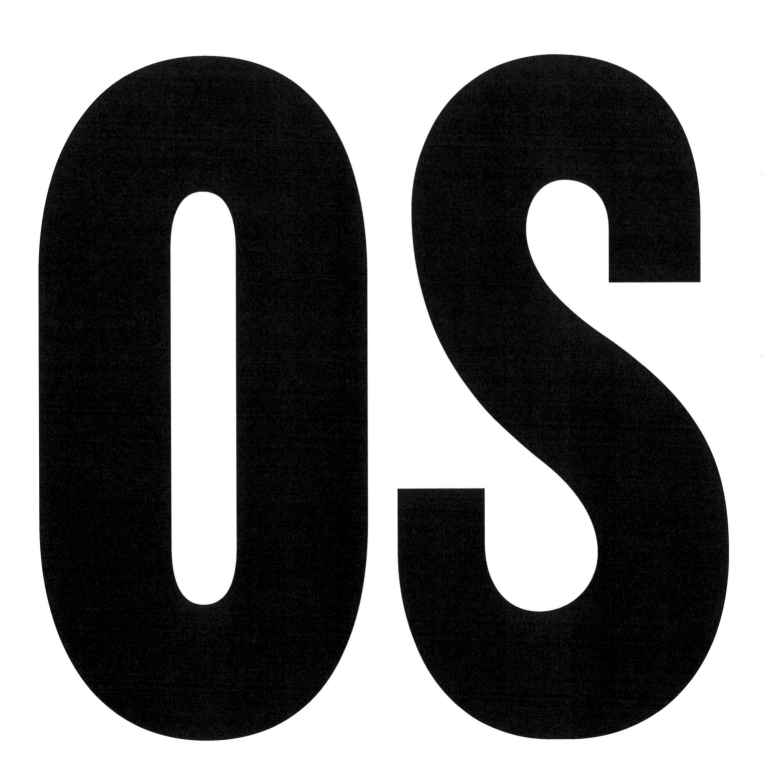

GLENN You grew up on the South Side of Chicago in a predominately black neighborhood. Your mother is white, and you've opened up about people mistaking your identity. How did people respond to you growing up, specifically when they saw you and your mom together, and what effect did that have on you and how you saw yourself?

YASHUA I didn't grow up with my dad, and there can be a different interpretation of being with my white mom versus being with another black family member. I grew up in a very proud predominately black environment, and I was surrounded by black empowerment. The South Side of Chicago was very progressive and a proud black cultural space. It included everything from the Nation of Islam, who have their headquarters in my neighborhood, to different grassroots organizations that were coming up in the '60s and '70s. Around my teenage years, it was difficult because, in many ways, you want to create an identity separate from your parents, and I think in some ways I resented my mother's whiteness because of the cultural space I was coming up in. It wasn't cool to have a white mom. I think I internalized that as it wasn't cool to be biracial. There was a tricky patch of time as I navigated some of that conflict. That was one aspect of being black that I think is pretty unique to the biracial experience. In some ways, you feel like you're not "black enough" for particular communities.

G When I reached out to you about possibly sharing some artwork for this project, you opened up about an assault at the hands of the police, and that you most likely would've been murdered had you not escaped. Can you speak about that experience?

Y I've begun to open up about that experience more recently because I've seen the value and impact opening up has had on me. Up until about a year ago, I hadn't connected the dots to how that experience affected me and my art.

That experience started with some knucklehead activity, with me and my guys hanging out outside of the club, waiting for some people to come out. We were being shoed away by security, and out of frustration, I kicked a construction horse that was nearby in the street, just being a rebellious teenager. After that, a car pulled up, and a guy rolled down the window and said, "I saw what you did. Get over here." It was an unmarked car. He didn't identify himself as police, and I didn't think he was a police officer, so I wasn't sure what was going on. He parked his car in the street, got out, and followed me. When I turned around and confronted him, a physical altercation happened. As we were scuffling in the street, more police cars with their sirens going pulled up. They jumped out and began to attack me as well. They cuffed me and put me in the car. Again, a plain-clothes officer in an unmarked car. I'm cuffed in the back of his car, and he's attacking me with one hand while driving the car with the other.

YASHUA KLOS
Pg. 153
Red Like Lightning, 2018
© Yashua Klos.
Courtesy of the artist and
Tilton Gallery, New York

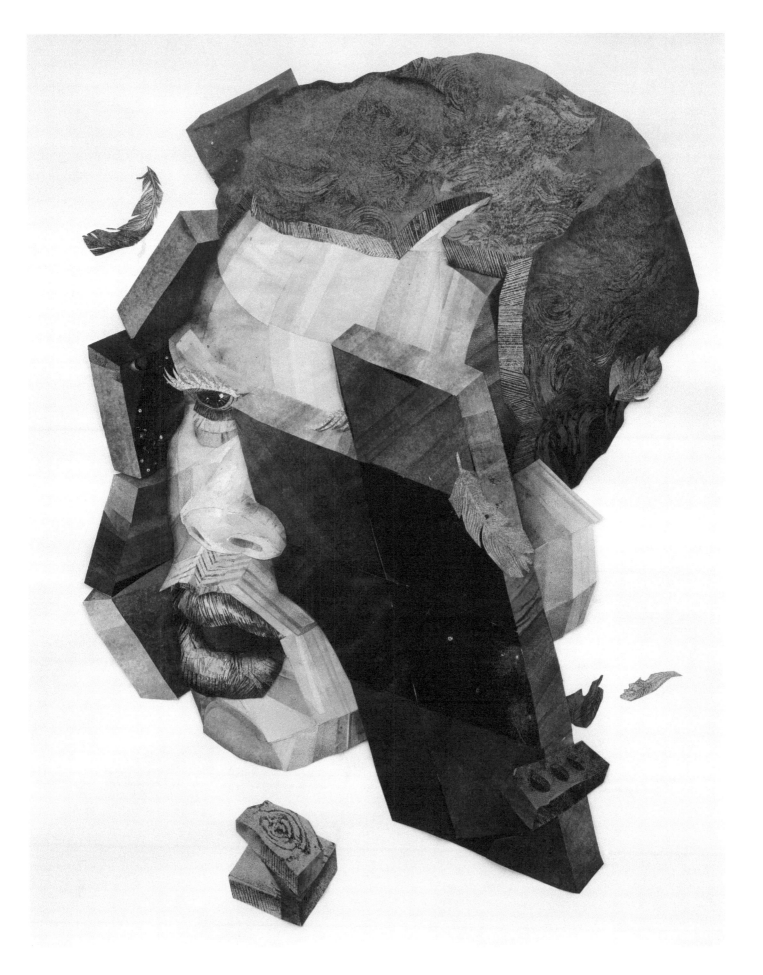

153

**TATENDA CHIDORA +
NAO SERATI**
TABLE SEAT, 2017
© Tatenda Chidora.
Courtesy of the artists

There were moments where I felt like I was blacking out in the backseat. Then, he parked the car, pulled me out, and started walking me toward an alley. It was about 3 a.m., and there was no one around. For a brief moment, he took his hand off of me. In that moment, I jetted and was able to escape. When I reflect back on that night, I don't know what his intentions were. He may have been intending to take the cuffs off of me and let me loose in the alley, but I wasn't about to find out because it hadn't been going my way.

G You've also opened up about your personal pain being a source of inspiration for your works, creating images that are in turmoil and existing in a state where they aren't "completely fixed and still in process." Can you speak about how that manifests in your practice?

Y I was fifteen at the time that happened and was still in high school. I was in this great advanced placement art class at the time and had this amazing teacher who saw something in me, even though I wasn't really applying myself in that class. The following week, we had a self-portraiture project, so I did a color pencil drawing with some collage in it. In it, I was still beaten from the incident but had this crown on my head of the Chicago skyline. It was a little cheesy, but it honestly captured how I was feeling about myself: a little sullen from the incident but also triumphant. I knew it was behind me, and I also accepted it as a part of being black and growing up in the city. In some ways, I even felt it was a rite of passage. That connects to the work I'm making now because the figures I'm making aren't fixed in any way; they're confronting challenges and negotiating their space against these very rigid structures. I'm depicting those structures as construction materials, whether they're 2x4s, bricks, concrete, and other building materials, which also represent the urban environment, the constructed environment that the black body has been quarantined to. They're navigating their survival and existence against a structure that is disallowing. There's a coexistence with that condition. I think about vines and how they crawl across a wall, merging with it, and I ask, "Would that vine be as successful in its growth if it weren't for that wall and that obstacle in front of it?" In a way, I'm thinking about the black figure in the urban environment as something that is resilient, just like that vine using the obstacles in front of it to be triumphant, to self-actualize.

G In addition to investigating these ideas and themes within the art, and subsequently finding healing there, what are some other ways you find healing and growth?

Y I believe in therapy, and it's been very beneficial for me to talk to someone without judgment, uncover subconscious thoughts, and put them into conscious words. I think my art helps me with that in a visual way, but doing it with language has been extremely helpful.

I'm also a big proponent of physical exercise as a way of squashing anxiety. I was reading the book *Post Traumatic Slave Syndrome* by Dr. Joy DeGruy, where she talks about how, generationally, African Americans have stored the trauma of the slave trade and all that's come with it in the body and the DNA. There's something we pass down genetically. I'm interested in the ways we can manage or overcome through exercise and physical exertion. So I run a lot and weight train and do martial arts, which has been freeing and a way to manage stress. I know everyone has their own thing, whether it's meditation or prayer, but my thing is exhausting myself so the voices of anxiety have less to hold onto.

G Another thing I wanted to ask you about is the investigation of blackness and black masculinity in your work, with collages being a practice in constructing a masculine identity. You've said, "There's no getting to the bottom of it." Can you speak about that investigation? Are you still investigating what that means within yourself?

Y When I talk about my work, I mainly use the word "deconstructing" rather than "constructing" because I think deconstructing is the act of taking what is available and what is already there and breaking it into its parts and reconfiguring them. That, to me, is the experimentation and investigation, moving those parts around and shifting them to see what holds up under pressure. When I say "pressure," I mean the environment I'm depicting, the pressure of those materials and the creative pressure I'm applying as an artist. I think what I'm discovering in each piece is how resilient blackness is. It's almost as if blackness in itself is a survival mechanism.

The *Shape Shifters* series are heads that confront a plane, and they're breaking through a plane, navigating around it, or even merging with it. When I started that series, I thought I'd only make maybe two or three of them, and here I am, a couple years later, having made almost a hundred. I've found so many ways in which the figure can exist and coexist with that pain and trauma. I've also found how it can deal with it, overcome it, or use it as a shield and hide behind it. It can wear it confidently, almost like an ornament, the way I was wearing that skyline crown in the first collage I did. I think that's what I'm discovering most in my process: how resilient blackness is. I think the essence of blackness may be adaptability; it may be this ability to shape-shift and survive by any means necessary.

I THINK THAT'S

DISCOVERING MOS

HOW   RESILIENT

I THINK THE ESSEN

MAY   BE   ADAPTA

BE THIS ABILITY TO

SURVIVE BY ANY M

WHAT I'M

T IN MY PROCESS:

BLACKNESS   IS.

CE   OF BLACKNESS

BILITY;   IT   MAY

SHAPE-SHIFT AND

EANS   NECESSARY.

RIC
KEY

LAURENTIIS

Rickey Laurentiis is a trans poet, author and teacher who does not identify as male. They have agreed to participate in this reflection of identity and masculinity, as they were assigned male at birth and presented as such in their past.

GLENN I read that, as a child, you began writing poetry for family and friends, but it didn't seem like it could necessarily be a career until you read Nikki Giovanni's *Cotton Candy on a Rainy Day*. With that said, when did you know this was what you wanted to do professionally, and was there pressure from family (or yourself) to pursue something "more realistic" or high-paying?

RICKEY I always knew. There was never a question of not knowing. I'm good at other things like the xylophone, and I remember my band teachers being mad that I didn't take their classes during my senior year. I was good at it, but I would have had to work harder. I have to work hard at being a poet, but it doesn't *feel* like work because I enjoy it. I love history too. If I had to have picked a scholarly pursuit, it probably would have been a historian.

G In your work, there seems to be a fascination with the human body, specifically the black body, and the violence that's committed against it. In "This Pair This Marriage of Two," you seem to reference cutting. Have you ever dealt with depression or self-harm?

R I tell people all the time that I've been sad. I have thrashed on the floor more recently, realizing I am trans and dealing with gender and the rationale that people don't really want to fuck with it, even though they still want to fuck. I'm like, "Oh, baby, pick one. You want to fuck me or fuck me up, or both?" So there are times I am literally thrashing on the floor, but I have never wanted to harm myself or end my life because of it. Y'all goin' to see me walk down the street, and y'all goin' to like it! I must have killed them just by walking down the street because that's sometimes enough to kill people. It was the same thing when I was a little boy in Catholic school. I always had some type of joy even though there was sadness floating around it. But I knew that was just what it was going to have to be. So either I am going to die from old age, the pandemic, or someone is just going to have to kill me because I am not going to kill myself.

G Following your work over the years, I've watched your evolution, having in the past referred to yourself as a black gay man to using #trans under selfies on your social media. I know there's a lot of young people and adults working through their identities and who they are. Can you speak about that journey?

R Well, I never referred to myself as a gay *man*. I just knew I wasn't a man. For me, names are important because names, as I often say, are gifts from your parents. Usually, it works out or we fix it, but sometimes it doesn't. I am not Matt. I don't want to be a Matt. The process of legally and socially changing your name is taxing and laborious. You have to really believe in it. I am a big fan and student of etymology. Go to names. org and search your name, and keep clicking until you get to the root because that is who you are. I even do it for people as a party game.

G There's another line from your poem "This Pair This Marriage of Two" that I'd like to read. "Must it be true that everything I make will be a self-elegy for what it fails to be?" Can you speak about that line?

R I tell people that book is relevant, but I wrote it a long time ago. Really, it's not that old; it came out maybe five years ago, but at that time, I thought the world was ending. There was a reason I completed those two because in my mind, they are twin poems. I shaped them that way so the stanzas could mirror each other. That poem is when I got tatted up! I have two tattoos across my body, and I am about to get a third one. They are both feathers. One is on my rib, and one is above my collarbone. I always wanted to put a tattoo there; it's very delicate. In that poem, I feel like I am describing the time I got the tattoo in St. Louis. I remember I was definitely going through something because I woke up and ran to the tattoo shop.

I remember reading Robert Hass's "Meditation at Lagunitas," and it talks about elegy. I can't really go back to then, but as I move forward, it brings to mind this notion that the very word itself is trying to capture what a table or a cat is. It's a possibility there is a failure, which is already dead. My cat just walks around me, and I call it my pussy, but even with slang, a pussy is not actually a vagina, a dick is not a dick, and a brick is not a brick. It almost makes fun of it or plays around with it. A thing cannot actually be what it is, so we may as well just call this "man." We may as well call this "dick" because it clearly is not dick, so that is kind of interesting to me. That space in between is kind of where I exist.

DEVAN SHIMOYAMA

Pg. 161
Oshun and the Pink Moon, 2020
© Devan Shimoyama.
Courtesy of the artist

161

Going back to that thought from earlier, I never really thought of myself as a gay man. I never thought of myself as a sad gay boy, although there are a lot. Most straight men are sad gay boys, so there are lots of them throwing all kinds of shit to numb themselves from the issues. There is a reason you have to repeatedly numb yourself. Pleasure is really good at that. It makes you really believe for one second that you can do this thing called life, then it's like the orgasm; you die right after. So I never thought of myself as a gay man because, frankly, I just accepted what people said, which was I am a man. Now, it's funny because when I say, "I am not a man; I am what I am," people say, "Oh, no, well, you can't be that." Oh, so you just want me to be miserable? Gotcha! I can't just pick the one I want to be? Before, they said I was a sissy and not a man. I was fine with that because if being a man means being like most men, I don't want to do that. I am OK being over here, doing me. That is what I was feeling there, and once I wrote it, my job was done. I can't tell you what it means, but I know what I was thinking about.

G Have you dealt with self-doubt or anxiety before showcasing your work to others, and if so, how do you overcome it?

R I have confidence, but I have so much doubt! Here is the thing: I'm not nervous when I self-publish something, which is why I tell my students to give themselves some space. If you are really doing the work, you are bringing it into the world. It's kind of like birthing a new child, and when you have a new child, you're not supposed to parade the baby around town for the first three months. So it feels the same way to me. Give yourself some time so when you do bring the child out or show the picture and announce the birth of your child, you are confident! You are the parent. You don't have time to be uncertain or doubtful. Those feelings will cause trauma where your child feels unworthy.

So that is how I feel. I do have lots of confidence. You have to find the confidence, and I've found it. I had posted maybe three pictures of myself on Instagram, and when I looked back at them, I understood why some girls didn't like me. I was over here doubting my body! That was the first time I had the courage to go all the way. I am not just trans; I am "whole trans." I chose to show my entire body, so there was nothing for anyone to use against me. That is my constant. There's a photo of me in a sports bra and panties. I was just in front of the mirror, and I wasn't trying to be sexual, but of course, it is going to be read that way. This is who I am, and if some fool is going to mock me for it, I don't see the point. You can't hurt me because I did it myself. You can't shame somebody with their own name.

Of course, I have doubt, especially when writing. I haven't finished my new book, but it is as large as my mouth right now for better or for worse. Equally, I think about the religion zoroastrianism, the Persian understanding of the God of Evil and the God of Good. They were always at war. That is how I feel. There is doubt and swag, swag and doubt. I go back and forth between the two. I say "swag" because confidence feels like the middle C to me. It is simple and calm. Doubt would be like trill versus swag. I can't live in the space of doubt or swag. They are both distortions of what reality is, and I would rather be half of each. I want to be content.

When you can just walk down the street and be content with the breeze hitting you in the face, that's love. When you are content and have an interior space you can go into, that's love. You might have a partner, and they also have an interior space they can go into. I'm tied to you, and you are tied to me. We can go to our interior spaces, then we can come out and have dinner together. When you are doubting yourself, I can help you, and when I am doubting myself, you can pull me back. We can balance each other out. This is becoming the philosophy.

G How did you become a teacher?

R I'm thirty-one, and I've always known I would teach. Wouldn't it be annoying if I wasn't a teacher? I would just be over here lecturing for no reason! I always knew this would happen. When my book first came out, I was at Columbia University. I wrote the book, and another poet named Timothy Donnelly was teaching at Columbia. You know how poetry works. People read your book, and sometimes they'll automatically say, "Yeah, that is a good poet. They should teach!" I could have been a horrible instructor. The field might want to rethink this philosophy because someone can write a good poem and be a great poet but not a good teacher. We've seen the results, and there's a history of that. I'm someone who is interested in intellectually educating in different frameworks. I'm very passionate about this work.

G You've had the opportunity to meet and converse with many brilliant writers over your career. Can you share any advice from your mentors or collaborators that has particularly affected you?

R One of my mentors is Carl Phillips; I just read his work. I remember reading his poem and not understanding it. Something about me said I didn't need to fucking get it. That's something people really have a problem with. I guess I have that kind of confidence where if I don't get something, I don't feel less than because of it. So I read the book, set it down, and was like, "I don't get this." I wasn't even articulate about it. Then, I went back to my life, went to the bookstore again, and saw him again. I only recognized his book because of a reading I had to do at Sarah Lawrence. He was the only black person, and I remember thinking he seemed sad. He had a soft sadness, and I didn't even recognize he was queer. He just seemed sad. That kept me going to his name, and I picked up another book *Speak Low,* and I didn't get it. I went to an earlier book, *The Rest of Love,* and this is the part of my logic where I like some of my classes on revision and where I feel like I have to read people's work in the order they wrote it.

So I read *The Rest of Love,* and I felt like a door opened. I felt a jolt. Then, I became completely lucid. The closest effect would be if someone studied a different language, and the moment they went to another country, they spoke the language fluently. But if I suddenly immerse myself in a new country and a different language, it would take about three months to experience the switch. But in that case, it's survival; you have to find where the bathroom is, find out what his name is, find out what the bill is, and you have to live. You don't have time to be scared. You can sit there and pee on yourself, or you can find the bathroom.

So to put yourself in that, the courage to sit in confusion momentarily, is actually like quarantine. It is a part of quarantine because you are uncertain, but you have a moment where you sit with yourself and make the decision to learn anyway. You can't just walk through Croatia and think you are going to speak fluent Croatian three months later. It felt like that. The language became immediately lucid, and I had enough of the stock to learn more. I began to understand this, and I could conjugate the verbs. I could learn the way we used to when we learned AAVE (African-American Vernacular English) as a small child.

This is the first trauma. I am glad we can block some shit because if we could go back to the world we used to have where everyone was trying to figure out what people are talking about, how scary would that be? We don't think of how terrifying that is. First of all, you were in your mother's womb. You thought that was the entire world, and you were content. All of a sudden, you slip out, something smacks you on the butt, and now, you're crying. Now you are in a whole new world. You are traumatized. That is trauma. You experience hunger for the first time, and you sip on something you later find out is the breast. That moment will later challenge you for the rest of your life.

G Being comfortable in the unknown.

R I did not make that up, but we have to keep saying that to the new people. We have to learn to be comfortable with the discomfort, which is another emotion or state of being. Sometimes we think only white people do certain things, but no, bitch, you logged onto Twitter today so you could complain about how overwhelmed you are with Twitter. "Oh, I just can't manage all of the images," like someone is holding a gun to your head. I am not trying to say there are not overwhelming images; all of that is significant, but you can log off. People don't want to log off, especially during the pandemic, because if they don't have a partner or live with someone, they have to be with themselves.

I love artists because we have experienced quarantine. That's our studio practice. That's our fellowship. We're constantly creating something new. We're constantly creating what interests us.

I AM NOT A MAN. I AM WHAT I AM.

MELO

LLOYD FOSTER

Pg. 170
Ghanaian-American II,
2019
© Lloyd Foster.
Courtesy of the artist

GLENN You were raised in the East Flatbush neighborhood of Brooklyn, and you've touched on growing up in a Jamaican home within your music. Can you speak about your parents and what kind of foundations they laid for you spiritually and musically?

MELO-X When my mom first came to this country, her, my aunts, and her friends were all in a choir. My mom and pops actually met in the church. My pops played some type of instrument (I think it was the tambourine), and my mom sang in the choir. So growing up, there was always gospel music playing in the house. I grew up around a lot of women, and they would always be singing these classic songs, songs I had never even heard of in other places, yet I had heard them sing them. That was very early, and for me, it was one of the biggest blessings I had as a child. You hear all of these stories about when you were a kid from the older folks who start reminiscing. So before I could even remember, I was in the church singing, and they said I would run up to the front and dance. I would raise my hands and try to sing the loudest. I remember seeing the Holy Ghost jump around people, and I would wonder why it wasn't jumping over me. I look back at those things now, and I'm like, "Oh, yeah. I was onto something." In any case, I had my own spiritual awakening when I was around fourteen, and I started studying Hebrew and the Torah. That was my own spiritual journey, but early on, there was a lot of gospel in the crib. My mom loved Al Green, Bob Marley, and old Jamaican hymns.

G One word that has been a through-line in your work is "God." Your catchphrase "It's the God, God" appears in many of your records, and it comes up in the title of songs, like "GODGOD" and "God Magic," as well as projects like *Mustafa The GodKing* and *GOD: Pièce de Résistance*. You've written about listening to that God, and tuning into your inner God to create your own destiny. Can you speak about connecting to that inner voice?

M As I get wiser, I understand more and more that everybody's path is different, you know? My journey is very different in terms of tapping into that. I think one of my first inclinations of mortality was when I was in Jamaica for a funeral at age three or four. Everyone was crying so hard, especially my mom. It was on a hill, and they had the casket on glass so you could see their face, and my mom was lifting me up to see the body, and I remember thinking, *What the hell is going on?* Seeing the body go down into the ground, that was the first time I can remember pondering death and feeling something around it. After that, I wasn't able to go to funerals for a while because I could just feel everyone's energy in the room. In "God Magic," I talk about when I almost drowned, and that was definitely another thing that made me question reality. When I was drowning, feeling like I couldn't breathe, I kept thinking I was about to die, and I began to see my life flash before my eyes. From an aerial view, I could see myself running around playing tag, which was all I did as a kid. I remember I began to question myself after that, and I began having these dialogues with God or the Universe.

I began studying Hebrew, which I think started because I was just looking for something. At the time, there was mad gang life in New York, and that was how my friend and I got drawn into it because it felt like a brotherhood. I say all that to say that it's a real individual journey dealing with God, spirituality and mortality. I think within all of that I realized the power of wanting to know more about life outside of what was being taught. At a certain point, I had read every book out there: the Bible, Koran, Book of Mormon, Book of the Dead. I just kept seeing a thread that connected all of them. When I put everything together, the main message was follow your gut. A lot of people think it's magic or witchcraft, but it is literally following your gut.

I can attest to that a lot because my spirituality comes from me empowering myself. In '07 or '08, I was doing research and listening to a lot of Wu Tang. They had a skit where they talked about God, and they were referring to God like "The God in me recognizes the God in you," and I was like, "Oh, this is the shit." So we started saying that in the hood, and I just ran with it. During my upbringing, I constantly questioned reality; everything I did was always with the intention of understanding more. Even when I was fairly certain about what I was going to do, I still questioned things, wondering where the loopholes were or what I still needed to learn.

WHEN I SEE MYSELF, I KNOW

I AM GOD,

AND I KNOW EVERY PERSON HAS THAT SAME ENERGY WITHIN HIM OR HER TOO.

I believe everybody's gut or inner voice sounds how it is supposed to sound to get through to that specific person. For me, I call them pings. Over the years, I've really studied myself, the dreams I had as a kid, and the power of words. As an MC and lyricist, you are constantly dissecting words and poetries. There are a lot of words I have learned from rap music. If I hear certain things or see certain words, I'm triggered to take action because I have been listening to myself and opening to the energy. I have this line where I say, "Look into the mirror and say hi to the Most High." When I see myself, I know I am God, and I know every person has that same energy within him or her too. Once I chose to operate in that mind frame, I had the most fruitful outcomes to my endeavors. It is training. I put ten thousand hours into production, working in FL Studio for days with no sleep. When I was younger, it was different, but now, I put in ten thousand hours of scribing. I write down all my dreams, and I have notes and symbols I have created for myself to remember certain shit. I have a system that works for me. It is like creating your own religion or spiritual practice. I make it work for me.

G In multiple interviews, you've described yourself as a writer first, and you've amassed writing credits on tracks like Beyoncé's "Hold Up" and "Sorry" from her *Lemonade* album. In those songs and on that album in particular, writing was cathartic and a way for her to not only express emotion and pain but also a way to understand her relationships and literally make lemonade when life gave her lemons. Can you speak a little more about the purpose writing serves in your life?

M My first piece of writing was a poem I wrote in junior high. I started writing poetry in the school yearbook. I was always into writing and seeing my thoughts on paper, even when I started writing more in my head. I had my own system of how I wrote my notes. Now, when I write, it just comes to me, and I'll write lyrics, poetry, and stories. I actually have been writing more children stories lately. I have one I am working on that talks about the aspects of sound to elementary children. When I have dreams, I always write them down. I used to record them a lot, but I write them down as well. When I get downloads of visions of the future, I will write that down too, so it is definitely cathartic in that sense. I really just flow freely and write down whatever. Sometimes it's just five words, and I really like those five words. I have a system that turns them into symbols and shit, so it's also cathartic in that sense.

G When did you begin meditating, and can you speak about what that practice looks like for you?

M Right now, where I am at, I understand that meditation is focus. We meditate all the time. Anytime you are doing some shit and your mind drifts off and you look and see three minutes has passed, that is meditation. It's when you focus your thoughts. My first time ever doing any kind of meditation was when I was a kid watching the first live-action *Ninja Turtles* movie. They were in the wilderness, and they were trying to find Splinter. Leonardo suggested that the group meditates so they can find him. They did it, and Splinter's spirit came up in the fire. He was blue, still alive, and they were able to talk to him. That really intrigued me as a kid, and that was the first time I started doing it. As a kid, I really liked the Ninja Turtles, so I would act like them and do what they did. That was my first time doing it without knowing what it was.

Another time I meditated without realizing it was when I would pray. I still pray, but when I was younger and studying a lot of Hebrew, I would pray and see that the things I asked for came to fruition. That in itself is meditation. Now I can sit and get into the zone wherever I am. I use it when my mind is cluttered or before I go to sleep. I like to rest my mind, and that's when I have more vivid dreams. I use it to help clear my mind because I'm scatterbrained, so it allows me to know where I am in the moment.

G You've been on a steady upward path in your career for over a decade. You've toured the world as a DJ, served as a sound designer for Jay-Z's 4:44 tour, curated live installations at MoMA and the Guggenheim Museum, and produced on Beyoncé's *Lemonade* and *BLACK IS KING*. On the road to get to where you are today, were there moments when you thought, "OK, I'm getting older? Maybe these creative pursuits are just a hobby. I'm not making the kind of money I'd need to support a family." If you did, how did you practice the patience necessary to stick it out?

173

M Yeah, man. For me, I would say that when I was really young, like in high school, I was very anti-music industry. I was into a lot of shit that was out, like Roc-A-Fella, Dipset, 50 Cent, and all that, but at the same time, I loved Rawkus, Pharoahe Monch, and Mos Def. It was funny. Around the time Nas' *Hip Hop Is Dead* dropped, I was into Madlib and MF Doom, and I learned about all of this alternative hip-hop that was still very much alive. It was thriving and crazy. I thought, *Yeah, hip-hop might be dead in a certain sense*, but I realized there were different frequencies out there. I learned about Tech N9ne and how he got the shipping, shirts, and CD cases, and he is one of the richest in the game, money-wise. So from that age, I was determined to make it on my own and do things how I wanted to do them. I was very hardheaded.

I'm very scatterbrained, and I wanted to create in so many different ways. I would make mixtapes, create the covers and mix the beats, and my boys were working with me. When I started DJing in the city more, I was also doing a lot of open mics. My goal was to make a living off of what I created. Anytime I felt like my work wasn't being recognized or the bills were stacking up, I would remind myself that I was still making a living off of what I created. I was doing a lot and was very in tune with the energy that various people needed me to do different things. The cover of my mixtape *Mustafa's Renaissance* was me sitting with the magazines I was into, the cameras I shot with, and other production tools that I used. Later, I identified as a multi-media artist; I do all of the different things. I didn't put myself in a situation where I wasn't going to love what I was doing. That meant I didn't move forward with certain labels or artists if I wasn't feeling it. I made sure I was always happy, and that is why, at a certain point, I was putting out mixtape after mixtape. Then, I got to a point where I was able to make the living I wanted to and spend time with somebody I loved. So now, I have built financial freedom through my creations and platform, and that's where I am now. I can stand on my own, balancing the different energies within myself, and my family can reap the benefits of my creations.

LAKIN OGUNBANWO

Pg. 175
Let It Be, 2016
Archival ink-jet print on
Hahnemühle Photo Rag
119 x 79.5 cm
© Lakin Ogunbanwo.
Courtesy of the artist
and WHATIFTHEWORLD

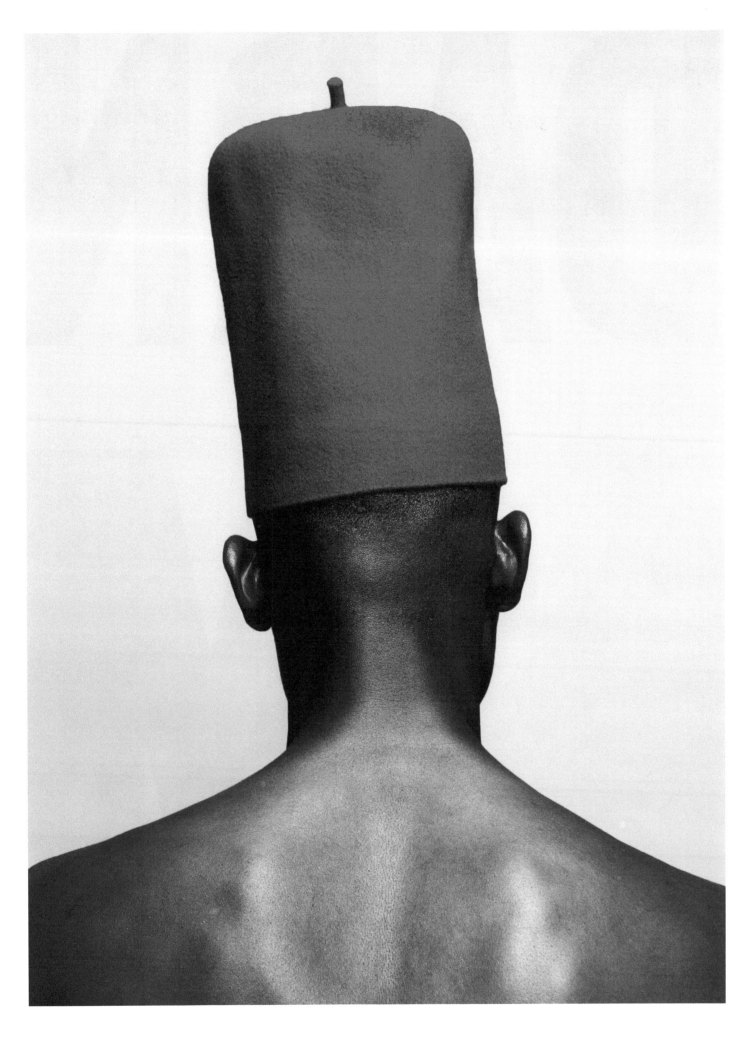

DARN

ELI L.

OORE

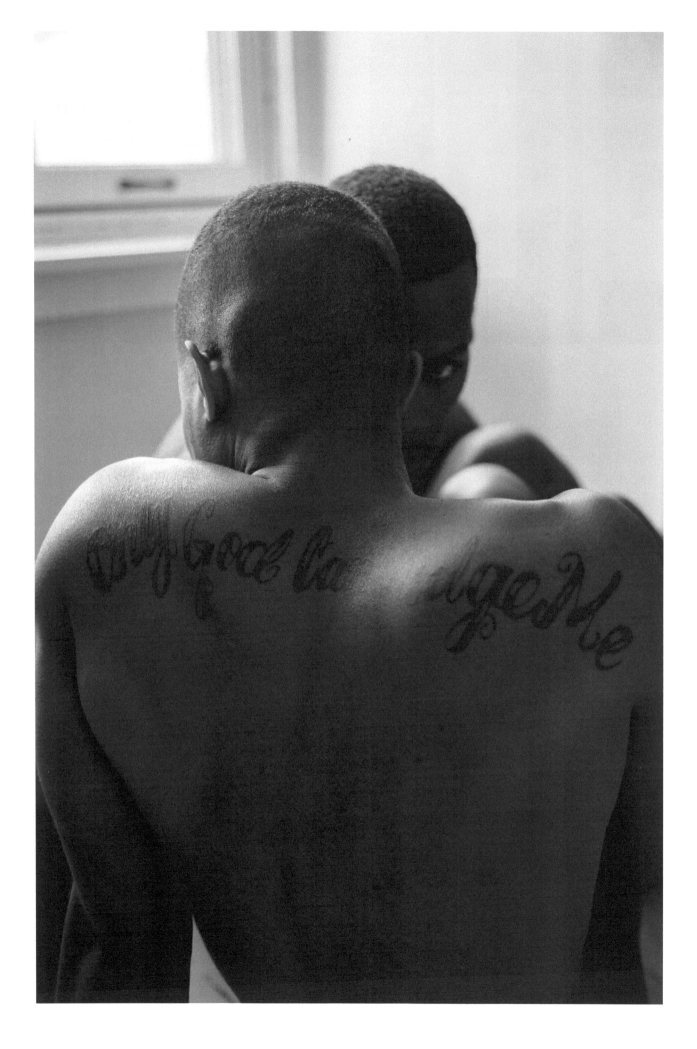

GLENN One thing that sticks out to me within your work is a proclivity for empathy. In your book *No Ashes in the Fire*, you speak frankly about your father and the abuse he inflicted on your mother, and yet, you chose to look deeper into him and his perspective, not justifying his behavior but examining and humanizing him. I'm curious about that philosophy and how it applies to your work as an activist. How do you see those intersecting?

DARNELL That is a good question. I am a firm believer in abolition as a practice, a politic, and a frank work. Inevitably, abolitionism and how I have come to think about it is based on a geographer named Ruthie Wilson Gilmore, who talked about abolition as not just the removal of the things that don't work for us (the institutions, systems, and in this case, practices) but an imagining of the things we need to build in place of those systems that don't work.

With that said, as someone who does not believe in prison or jails, which have been the source of long-standing problems in inequity in the US, and as a person who is concerned about the way punishment is used to solve complex issues, I can't resort to punishment or practices of harm as the go-to for ending conflict. As it relates to my family and my father, I came to realize that prisons are not the solution, nor is punishing people in a death chamber.

What does this mean in terms of my relationship with someone who is harming my life? I'll give you an example of justice from the perspective of my mom and my dad, where violence was very much a part of their relationship. Justice for me looks like calling a safe number that was set up by me, my mother, and her family members instead of calling the cops. If there was any indication that Daddy was about to act up, we could call the safe number and get to the house to 1) make sure my mother is safe and 2) de-escalate him and get him out of the house. Maybe we could call a healer or spiritualist. Maybe one of those people would be a mental health specialist who could give him the support he needed while out of the house so he was not harming my mom and also not in jail. This would allow him to safely get the help he needed to unlearn all of the things he may have thought were true of manhood, masculinity, and power.

The last thing I will say is writing about my father was easy. It's easy to talk about him, even though he's seen as a monster with a capital M. That view of him really allowed me to distance myself in a sane way. The form of socialization that shaped me is the same thing that shaped him. He came to be who he was because he believed in the power of sexism and the patriarchy, and so did I at one point. It's important to humanize him, as he did both good and bad, *and* to hold him accountable. At the same time, I must be self-reflective, and I can't let myself off of the hook as an innocent bystander who was not ready to take accountability for my life.

G You've also written candidly about depression and the suicidal thoughts you had while at Princeton Theological Seminary. Can you speak about that time and how you survived that dark patch?

D The days I maneuvered through depression were probably the darkest days of my life. I don't know if you've experienced this, but the sun would be out and it would still feel like a dark day outside. In some ways, I look back, and I actually —this sounds a bit existential— was kept by a spirit and the love of my friends and family. They may not have had the words to say what they were thinking, but they saw me struggling with a dark period of my life and showed up anyway.

What's interesting is that I was determined to take myself out of there. Part of it had to do with how I was shaped by my religious teachings. Growing up, I had been told I was going to Hell. Since I was walking around believing there was a God that damned me, it certainly made sense why I felt like I didn't deserve to be here. Part of getting free from that was unlearning and doing away with the messages I had received and literally loving myself more than I loved some human's creation of God, and that was a lot of fucking work. I had to reject years and years of conditioning. I had to leave my church and turn my back on so much of what I put my faith into and believed in. I remember looking in the mirror one time and thinking of everything I had been taught to hate about myself. It was hard for me to look in the mirror sometimes. I couldn't look at my big lips, couldn't look at my skin color, and I couldn't look in my eyes because I would only see the reflection of the person who was hiding inside. One day, I had to look inside and say, "I love all of you." That was a moment of salvation for me. I also give a lot of credit to my mother, who affirmed my being at twenty-eight years old and said, "You deserve to be here, and I love you." In that moment, it was like shackles broke off of me, and it really gave me the courage to keep going.

G Do you remember where you were physically, mentally, and spiritually when you decided to write *No Ashes in the Fire*? What were your intentions and hopes for the work, and who was the book intended for?

D I did a big bulk of the writing in a two-story house I rented in College Park in Atlanta. It was a senior care home, and I knew nothing about Atlanta, but I traveled down there by myself. I wrote for three months in that house, and it was like a crucible, to use Baldwin's words. I felt like I was thrown into a room with memories I had worked so hard to put aside, but I had to confront them. I was thrown into the room with myself, and I had no choice but to sit with myself and reflect. My father passed as I was writing the book so I was in that house mourning and grieving through the writing process. I was completely alone for the most part.

I spent eighty-five percent of the time by myself; I would only go out on the weekends. I would describe the entire process as a breaking, like literally breaking. I feel like I was putting aside words and breaking apart my relationships, but by the end, I had experienced something of a life transformation. I was different, and I often say, even now as I am working on this second book, it is so hard to get back into the flow of writing. Now, I know what it takes to get it done. I tell my publishers that I know I am way behind, but once you commit and start that process, you are jumping right back into the breaking. I was a different person by the end of writing that book, and maybe that is part of the process. I came out changed and on the other side of it.

G Can you speak about your second book?

D The second book is different. It isn't a memoir. Sometimes you get book proposals that are very grand, and you're like, "How the hell am I going to do this?" This is one of those projects! I am supposed to write a creative non-fiction book that's

tentatively titled *Visions: Unbecoming Visions Beyond a Manhood*. The central argument is that instead of encouraging men to believe being a "real man" is better, we should encourage everyone to be their true selves. My liberation in life has come from failing at or not conforming to the things I was told I had to become to be an "acceptable man." I am trying to piece together chapters that invite the reader to unlearn the idea that gender, whether manhood or womanhood, was made for us. It's a cage on the route to freedom. It seemed easier to do when I was writing the proposal. I still have to figure out what that concept will look like. We'll see how it goes!

G What do you think are some things that can be done to shape a freer tomorrow and get out of the "cage of masculinity?"

D There are a couple of things. The first is to unlearn, but to do that, we have to know we are in a cage in the first place. The book will help to reveal or reiterate what that cage is, the lessons we are taught as children, the influences of masculinity and manhood, patriarchy, and sexism, and all the rules we subscribe to and breathe like air. Basically, you're born and the doctor smacks your butt and says, "It's a boy" before you can even speak. This whole announcement has been made on your behalf. Is that freedom? You never get a chance to determine who you want to be, *how* you want to be. So a big part of the first part of the book is unpacking that.

The second and third parts offer scenarios of what that might look like in intimate relationships, say with men who are not identified. I have a friend who is not gay and doesn't identify, but we have one of the most intimate, closest relationships I have ever experienced, even closer than a relationship I have had with a "woman." It felt radical and beautiful because it wasn't trapped in these identifiers. I was shaken by it and had to tell myself, "Wait, this isn't gay. This is just what it means to be humans who are actually showing up, making space, and opening their hearts to intimacy." What if you were able to have that without it being attached to a scandalized thing? How many of us would be having free relationships with other men and other people in general? How many of us would ask for a hug when we really needed one?

PEOPLE'S STORIES
MATTER, ESPECIALLY WHEN

THERE'S BEEN A DEATH CHAMBER

ENCASING SO MANY OF OUR
NARRATIVES.

G What would you tell a young person who is asking if they should write a memoir or "does my story matter?"

D Yes! People's stories matter, especially when there's been a death chamber encasing so many of our narratives. You know history does not tend to be very kind to those who have been on the underside of power. Every opportunity we have to write our stories is a pushback. It doesn't matter who refuses to center black people's stories, queer people's stories, any of our writing. We're still going to be writing anyway. How powerful is that?

G How has your idea of God transformed? Do you consider yourself a "believer?"

D At the seminary, I came to realize that even if the Bible ceased to exist, there is a presence of spirit that is so far beyond our comprehension —or at least the way we try to water down the comprehension for human understanding. Whether God is in the collective presence of an ancestral force or the presence of spirit, I don't know, but I am a church boy at heart. Even outside of church, I have experiences that are life changing. Even beyond the amazing things outside of my life, what I might call miracles, I can't help but look at the world we live in. Every day, I look outside and think *How the hell am I here?* Looking at the magic of science is dope. Sometimes I shift my perspective outside of this world and think about how small the confines of Earth are and how big the universe is, and I get so dumbfounded by the limitations of my under- standing. I can't help but preach to something other than us, something other than myself. I still pray; I pray with fervency, and I still give thanks. I won't stop that, but it has also been in a way that has allowed me to be free of manmade theologies that tell you God is supposed to love a particular kind of person and not our wide array of expressions. God to me is one of justice, and that is my theology.

Pg. 183
Caretaker, 2019
© John Singletary. Courtesy of the artist and Black Art In America

MIKE

GLENN In your music and work, you open up about your anxiety and depression. You have your hand in a plethora of projects, from *The New Negroes* to *Call & Response* to performing on stage and acting. What does that anxiety look like in the midst of your work, and how do you address and overcome it?

OPEN MIKE EAGLE For me, I like to compartmentalize, as it allows me to not fully feel the anxiety so I can focus on whatever I need to focus on. The con is I often feel like I don't have the space to connect with my feelings. In the long run, this is something I am working to undermine in my therapy work. My compartmentalization is a lot less front brain; it is so learned that I'm just focusing on whatever is in front of me. That feeling is there; it just doesn't connect to my front brain so it sits in my body until it's processed. Because of this, I'll have random anxiety attacks based on something I have previously felt. I didn't give myself enough space to feel.

G In the early stages of your career, what did depression look like during the grind, and how did it affect your journey?

O I can't say I fully understood my feelings at the time. I don't think I was really aware. I had been operating in a depressed state for so long, I barely knew any other way. I was just creating with that energy the entire time. In the beginning of my career, I would meet people and build a working relationship that seemed good, but when I submitted my work, I would stop hearing from them. It really bothered me. To this day, I feel I am sensitive to it because of how things were early on in my career. I still haven't quite figured out how to deal with the stuff I was dealing with then.

G Looking back at that time in your life, was there ever anger toward those people or bitterness you had to address?

O I don't know, man. I've always swallowed it, and I'm still figuring out how to stand up for myself. I can remember times when I was a little too standoffish or a bit passive aggressive in business relationships. I think it's because I'm still learning all the things I didn't know how to do. Sometimes I would feel disrespected, and figuring out what to do with my feelings in those moments has been a journey. There is a lot of trash involved when trying to sell art, especially if it's a way that doesn't offer a lot of resources. It can be rough. You can end up taking it personally, and there isn't a manual for how to handle it. Nobody can tell you what you need to do to feel better.

G Do you meditate?

O Yes, I've meditated on and off for years. I've been heavily involved with it and have completely lost it at other times. I think the happy medium is just being mindful, even if that means simply adjusting my breathing. I don't have a mindfulness practice per se, but being aware is the key.

G What does depression look like for you in your daily life?

O Mine is like a permanent low-grade, functional depression. I don't mean permanent as in I'm always going to feel that way, but permanent in the sense that it is an everyday thing. When I had times I couldn't function, it was maybe over the course of three hours. Everything just bubbled up to the surface, and I couldn't do anything but cry. There was nothing else to be done. It's like lava that boils under the surface; occasionally the pressure builds up and it has to erupt. It never happens for very long though, and I find that I have to process and sit with those things; otherwise, I won't be able to function.

G During an interview with John Moe, you alluded to a specific trauma in your childhood and how it affected you in so many aspects of your life. So many of us have experienced things we never should have as kids, and subsequently, when we have kids, we stress or worry about them excessively. Have you found that's shaped you at all as a father and protector?

O With my kids, specifically? Yeah, I find I am overprotective for sure. It is exactly because of that. I'm hypersensitive to him being in any situation where something could happen to him, and I have to work toward letting him be. It's a very front brain nightmare to imagine something will happen to him because something happened to me.

G Shifting gears toward your career, do you remember a time where everything began to change for the better?

I cherish my sleep.

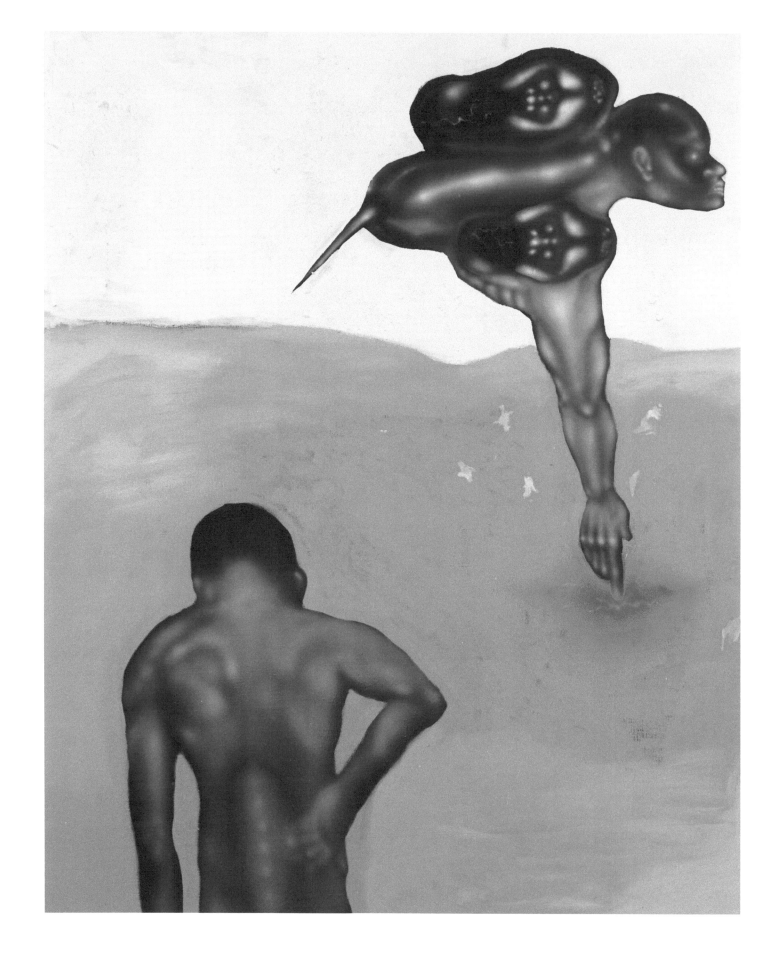

I WAS WAITING ON A SINGLE MOMENT TO HAPPEN THAT WOULD MAKE EVERYTHING EASIER, BUT IT TURNED OUT THAT THINGS HAVE GOTTEN <u>EASIER</u> FOR ME OVER TIME BECAUSE OF ALL THE DIFFERENT THINGS I'VE BEEN ABLE <u>TO DO.</u>

O I came into music logically, thinking there were things that would be game changers, and I was always trying to maneuver myself toward those things and experiences. I had to learn that kind of thing doesn't exist for me; it may exist for some people but not for me. I'm just not the type who has the single moment where everything changes. I am a drop in the pop culture bucket. Everything drops into a bucket, and maybe one day the thing tips, but maybe it doesn't. I have had to think of it that way. That was one of the reasons I was constantly frustrated; I was waiting on a single moment to happen that would make everything easier, but it turned out that things have gotten easier for me over time because of all the different things I've been able to do.

G On your web series *Call & Response*, you speak to a lot of different people, black collaborators specifically, about these times and the changes we are demanding. Having spoken with so many different people, has there been anything that has stuck out to you, and are you positive about the future with everything you've talked about and heard?

O I truly respect all of the people we talk to. Some of the questions I ask them come down to what we've been talking about here: being mindful, taking the time to unplug and breathe correctly, and the kind of focus and presence of mind those things can create in people. I admire that so much, so I think a lot of my questions were trying to get at that, and it resulted in the same answers: people taking time to pull their brain away from all of the noise and self-reflecting about their mental health. The takeaways for me were mostly about the mindful, sensitive individual and how they move through these waters while taking the time to treat themselves well.

Another thing is that, when one of our brothers or sisters gets murdered by the police, we sometimes think we are the only ones who experience that trauma, but it isn't just us. I think it is us more acutely, but I think we all sit under this American lie of equality for all. Capitalism leads us to believe our happiness makes us important, especially when we watch somebody's life get taken away like that. It kills the dream for everybody. You can rationalize it all you want, but deep down, everybody knows that if that can happen to one of us, it can happen to anybody for any reason. I think that's why we're seeing a lot of people step up. We are not the only ones experiencing that trauma. Like I said, we definitely feel it the most, but other people feel it too. They feel that betrayal, and they know if it is not because of their skin color, it could be because of their gender, sexual orientation, socioeconomic class, etc.

RASHID JOHNSON
Pg. 191
Untitled Anxious Red Drawing, 2020
Oil on Cotton Rag
60 x 40 in
© Rashid Johnson.
Courtesy of the artist

MARCO

194

GERALD CYRUS

Pg. 194
Wali, 2001 – 2008
© Gerald Cyrus.
Courtesy
of the artist

GLENN You grew up in North Memphis, Tennessee, in an area you've described as "hyper-violent." You've lost good friends and were exposed to murder literally at your doorstep. Do you remember being that age? How were you processing those tragedies?

MARCO I do remember being that age, but I don't think I was really processing it at that time. It just felt like a normal, day-to-day thing, and it seemed as if it was supposed to be happening. I was trying to make sense of it. At that age, I was also trying to use it as an internal badge of honor, if you will. "This is the environment I'm coming up in, but it ain't happening to me." I lived with that type of energy and vibe. Walking around the neighborhood made me a little more scared, especially when I thought about it happening right on my doorstep. It made me much more aware of my environment, but I didn't truly process that event until later when I was in high school.

G During your TEDx Talk, you spoke about being the youngest of four and how your mother was forced to leave due to the abuse from your father. Can you speak about getting through that time and how you felt about your father, your mother, and her leaving?

M It was tough to understand because my dad wasn't just the man who let this happen; he was my dad. For years, he tried to paint my mom as the villain and the person who left us. I really had to battle internalizing those ideas about my mom. For me, my relationship with her has really allowed me to tap into my spirituality more because I've always felt her energy. Even when we weren't living in the same house, I always felt her support and prayers. From day to day, I had to constantly remind myself that my mom was dealing with mental health issues that were not entirely caused by my dad but, in many ways, were exacerbated by him.

G You've told the story multiple times about a instance in 2009 when you and a friend were playing with a gun. It almost went off in your face, and you've said, "That was the day I said I'm done messing around with the hood shit." Can you speak a little about your life at that point and what you were into? Did you have a vision for your future before that incident?

M Yeah, my vision before that time was strictly based in music. I had been making music for about four years prior to that incident. I was always thinking about music. I used to have these note-books where I'd write the name of my record label at the top of the paper with my album and song titles listed. I had been doing that since about fifth grade. When this incident happened in 2009, I was in tenth grade. I had been thinking about music, but I was dealing with so much emotional damage, including an abusive household that included sexual violence, and I was acting out. I was participating in activities that weren't the best for me, but I did have a focus on music.

I was in high school during an era where there was an influx of Teach for America teachers, so they were letting go of all the older teachers with seniority to make way for younger teachers, many of whom were twenty-five to thirty years old. Those teachers became my first test market, my first fans, people I knew would purchase my music. I had been thinking about music on a day-to-day basis while simultaneously participating in street shit, trying to be macho. The only reason we had the gun in the first place is because we wanted to feel tough. The day the gun almost went off in my face was an eye-opening experience. At the time, I had a 1.7 GPA, and at the rate I was going, I wasn't going to graduate high school. I decided to become my own guidance counselor in a way. I was smart and tested into all the advanced placement classes before I even made it to high school. So I decided to apply myself. I got into all honors and AP classes and raised my GPA to a 3.0 in two years. I kept focusing on the music too.

G You've traveled to Bolivia with the Next Level Program, served as a member of the Memphis Music Initiative, collaborated with Black Lives Matter on your *Grc Lnd* project, and sat as the artist in residence at Georgetown University. Was there a moment in your career when its trajectory and the reason for making music began to shift for you?

M Yeah, that shift came in high school as well. There was a traumatic moment I experienced with my dad. I had two mixtapes I was putting out, two terribly recorded mixtapes, but I had fans, so what did it matter? I had about seventy-five to one hundred CDs pressed up and ready to go. My dad listened to one of them, took all of my tapes, and told me I couldn't put it out because of what I was talking about. I'm not saying what he did was right, but it forced me to rethink how I was telling stories. It forced me to ask myself, *Do I always want to be the first-person shooter or the person committing these proverbial crimes in the songs I'm making?* By the time I got out of high school, I had made a dramatic shift.

CHOOSING LOVE
THING I HAD TO
IS   A CHOICE.
LOVE EVERY DAY,
ON IT
NOT SOME FAIRY

IS THE MAIN

<u>LEARN.</u> LOVE

YOU CHOOSE TO

AND YOU WORK

EVERY DAY. IT'S

TALE THING.

I was also struggling with the idea of going to college and working these jobs. People were constantly asking me, "What's your backup plan?" All of those things forced me to think about how I could do music in a bigger way. Jay-Z and Yo Gotti were my role models at the time, so I realized I could do something bigger. One pivotal moment for me was a high school project I participated in called the Capstone Project, where I learned about infant mortality in Memphis. I found out the infant mortality rate within certain zip codes in Memphis is higher than the infant mortality rates in places like Sri Lanka and Iraq. Learning about environmental injustice was a big thing for me as well.

G You're married to Dr. Zandria Robinson, an artist in her own right and assistant professor of sociology at Rhodes College. Was there any programming you had to unlearn or hurdles you had to jump through regarding relationships, marriage, and being a married man on the road?

M Yeah, the first layer of programming is what we talked about, looking at my dad and mom. My dad demonized her and her mental illness, as well as the institution of marriage. I was definitely coming into the relationship with a fear-based, scarcity mindset. I consciously had to unlearn that. It was like a pastime in my childhood home to speculate who would get a divorce first. I remember my father lost a bet because he predicted Will and Jada were going to get divorced in the early 2000s. Even when my uncle got married, my dad said, "Oh, now you know this ain't gonna last." So I had to unlearn being skeptical of love and marriage.

Another difficult layer for me personally is that my wife is ten years older than me. That's a stigmatized thing, and back then, I felt so unworthy because the money wasn't coming in, and I wasn't established. When I met my wife, I felt like I was at a low point because of my financial standing, not even really factoring in my mental health. Choosing love is the main thing I had to learn. Love is a choice. You choose to love every day, and you work on it every day. It's not some fairy tale thing. I had to ask myself, *Do I want to spend another ten years doing young-folk bull crap, or do I want to build some type of stability for my family, myself, and my community so I can be a better member of society?* My focus was on making a marriage work at twenty-two years old.

G With everything you've been through, have you dealt with depression, anxiety, or methods of escapism? Are you still a practicing Muslim?

M That's a wonderful question. To answer the first part, yes. I've dealt with depression, was diagnosed with generalized anxiety disorder (GAD), and have had my run-ins with the Zolofts and Buspirones of the world. Those came with some of the experiences I had dealing with an abusive father. After leaving the house, I moved back in with my father, and it was a really rocky period. In retrospect, I could sense the abuse and anger rising to the point where if I hadn't left the house again, something bad would've happened. He probably would've killed me. So 2012 to 2014 was a really traumatizing time in my life. Most days, I was living out of a brown paper sack. One of the best decisions I continued to make was choosing music, and in choosing music and myself, I was able to meet my wife, my life partner.

In December of 2013, I was working a temp job, and I remember thinking to myself, *When this job is over, I am never doing this again. I don't know how I'm going to make this work, but I know I'm never working at a place like this again.* Around that time, I had come across *As a Man Thinketh*, which helped me start thinking independently and striving to bring positivity into my life. I had started reading more books like that, and I wrote down this manifesto, my creed, basically what I wanted to do. I wrote down my music goals, and that change started with blind faith in myself to make this happen. I began to accomplish things within the music arena that gave me more confidence. Once I met my wife, she introduced me to a lot of new ways of thinking and more books to read.

At that time, I was struggling a bit with my identity as a Muslim and what it meant to be Muslim. In these monotheistic religions, there's always a punishing God. Subscribing to that made me feel like I was always doing something wrong. Once I got married, I came back to Islam by practicing Ramadan, and my wife was simul-taneously introducing me to different African spiritual practices. I was introduced to the Orishas, and that helped me a lot too. I met with a spiritual coach, and she informed me my mother goddess was Oshun, so for a long time, I'd light the candles on my Oshun altar every Friday. I even got a tattoo of Oshun on my forearm!

A big thing for me was starting to attend therapy in 2016. Therapy, in conjunction with my spiritual practice and investigating my faith and relationship with religion, was a powerful thing for me. But being in a partnership with someone who has your back, who sees your struggles, knows your pain, but who also has their own pains, allows you to comfort them and that has really helped me. I had to unlearn a lot and tap into a new energy.

PHIL

ROWAN

RICARDO

LIPS

202

Pg. 202
*Well, Well, Well
(Chiffon In Green),*
2020
© Dominic Chambers.
Courtesy of the artist

GLENN As a writer, you move between styles including poetry, screenwriting, art critique, sports writing, etc. Can you speak about being a young poet and coming out of college? Did you imagine your career would look like this?

ROWAN No, I didn't imagine it would look the way it does now because I didn't have an endgame. I really have a certain belief of life, and it starts with the goodness of the arts and humanities and immersing yourself in that, no matter what you do. When I graduated from college, I knew I wanted to write, and I knew I *would* write, but I didn't think about it in terms of "I should go to graduate school" or "I should be a professor of English literature." As a matter of fact, I went to grad school because I still had a lot of questions about poetry and art, and I thought that would be the best thing to do: spend six years or so digging into the crates, which is what I consider libraries and archives to be. From there, my plan was to let it be what it will be. If I am someone else with a PhD in English literature, so be it, but I was young; I graduated when I was twenty-one and went straight to grad school.

Toni Morrison had a full career as an editor and wrote her first book, *The Bluest Eye,* at forty years old. I was really comfortable with the idea of art being a long game, and the long game is the only game there is. I could do anything and write poetry. My work in grad school worked out for me, and I had opportunities in academia I could take. I taught at Harvard for my last year of grad school, and I had an opportunity to move back to New York and go to Stony Brook, which is not in the city but close enough. You know how rare it is to be in academia and live in New York? I have to say, it helped me out a lot because Stony Brook is an hour-and-a-half away from New York, so I would go there to teach, but outside of that, I had my own life as a writer making my way.

G When receiving the 2019 PEN/ESPN Award for Literary Sports Writing, you stated, "Action's the only testament for moral behavior, and writing's the only action that I know..." Can you speak about that quote, what it means to you, and the importance of writing in times like these?

R Michael S. Harper shared that James Baldwin quote with me. I have never found it as a quote for him, but I can see him saying it. I have a strong ethical sense in my work, and I always want to do the right thing in the right moment. I don't know if it is important to write in these times. I think it is OK sometimes for the writing to not come out. It is OK to not be ready to respond in a particular moment as a writer. What is most important is the humane aspect that brings us to writing. I like to think that instead of calling all the poets and painters when shit is going down, we act as sponges. The world is complex, and these moments are incredibly complex, and writers are processing these complexities in a way that has a strong ethical component to them. Now, ethical doesn't mean it's the nicest thing to do or say.

No, it is about when you put the words or the art down, whether it is plastic or conceptual, do you believe in it and mind the complexities? I have gotten to the point where the only definition of poetry that really satisfies me is that poetry is something that sounds good and is something you believe in. I know that sounds simple, but it is really hard. It is easy to write something that sounds good, but do you believe in it? At the end of the day, do you stand by what you said? It is also easy to write things you believe in, but does it sound good and find that balance?

Robert Hayden has a poem about Frederick Douglass that ends with, "this man, superb in love and logic, this man shall be remembered. Oh, not with statues, rhetoric, not with legends and poems and wreaths of bronze alone, but with the lives grown out of his life, the lives fleshing his dream of the beautiful, needful thing." For me as a writer, I am always thinking about what is beautiful and what is needed and trying to nestle somewhere between that. George Floyd's last words were to his dead mother. You need your mother, whether she is in the physical form or in the ether. You call for her, and that is the real spirit of love that I look for in my writing, as well as other writing genres.

G I came across a pretty nasty review of *Living Weapon* in *The New York Times*. Does a review like that irk you?

R I had a good laugh about it. That guy is known for those kinds of reviews, and it was pretty bad. My editor had a good laugh and said, "You made it!" Anybody who takes that guy's unadulterated nonsense as fact, more power to them. I didn't worry about it too much, but I did find myself wondering why *The New York Times* assigned someone who is known for slagging off on writers. Better to let another poet review it than to waste time and space in that way. This is the casual type of racism masking itself as critical assessment that has been plaguing writers and artists for a long time.

Toni Morrison once wrote about how the goal of racism is to distract us from our work. I am not distracted, and I find that I am very comfortable where I am as a writer. I'm not complacent, but I have been fortunate to have never received a poor review in my life. This was the first one, and I would welcome it if I could learn something from it. I am an artist, and I want to learn. Criticism is a part of that, but when I read it, there was nothing going on there. It was entirely subjective without any critical engagement. If there's something in there I could learn from, then I would take my lumps and grow from it. There are certainly reviews that rub you the wrong way, but this wasn't one of them.

THE ONLY DEFINITION
OF POETRY THAT
REALLY SATISFIES ME IS THAT

POETRY

IS SOMETHING

THAT
SOUNDS
GOOD

AND IS
SOMETHING YOU
BELIEVE IN.

I got a great review of *Living Weapon* in *The Los Angeles Times* by a young critic I didn't know. It is better you don't know who is critiquing you, but there are critics who have been in the game for a while, and you end up knowing who they are. *The Los Angeles Times* wrote a wonderful review, and even thought it isn't one hundred percent positive, it was overwhelmingly so and had a refreshing level of engagement. There were little critiques here and there, but that's what critics are supposed to do.

G You've mentioned stargazing in multiple interviews and lectures in the past. Can you speak about the importance that stargazing has in your life and what it brings up within you?

R I've always been captivated by skylines and starscapes, and the phenomenology that the light of the sun is dead light that arrives eight minutes after it's produced. As a city kid, I was always trying to hammer down this idea that I wasn't divorced from nature. There is a romantic idea that you could escape the city to find nature. I grew up watching those phenomenal sunsets behind buildings in the Bronx and skyscrapers in Manhattan. I remember seeing the East River, the planes flying over La Guardia, the leaves changing, cracks in the concrete with dandelions and weeds popping up, and all of that to me was nature. You give me some music and a chance to sit and look at the sky, and I am gone. I can do that all day every day. I feel like it is the great work of art we are a part of. The great concept and phenomena of the sky is endless, deep, and completely intangible, yet it feels tactile. We breathe it in, yet we can't exist in the stratosphere.

To me, it's the first encounter with the imagination. All of my art comes from these types of encounters, whether you are listening to classical or jazz or just having deep thoughts. It is the music of the sphere; it is where our idea of harmony comes from. The sky is capacious enough to hold all of these styles at once, whether it's Bach writing from the heavens or George Clinton in outer space. All of this is in the sky, and to me, it is the great egalitarian artist, if you will. When you look out at the sky, it is capacious enough and unbiased enough, savage enough and chill enough, to handle all our complexities. I like to have moments where I can be in silent communication with it. That is where all of the art comes from for me, all of the imagination. It keeps me sane.

GRANVILLE CARROLL

Pg. 207
Interbeing, 2020
From the series
*Because The Sun Hath
Looked Upon Me*
© Granville Carroll.
Courtesy of the artist

BROD

PURE

ITEZ

IELL

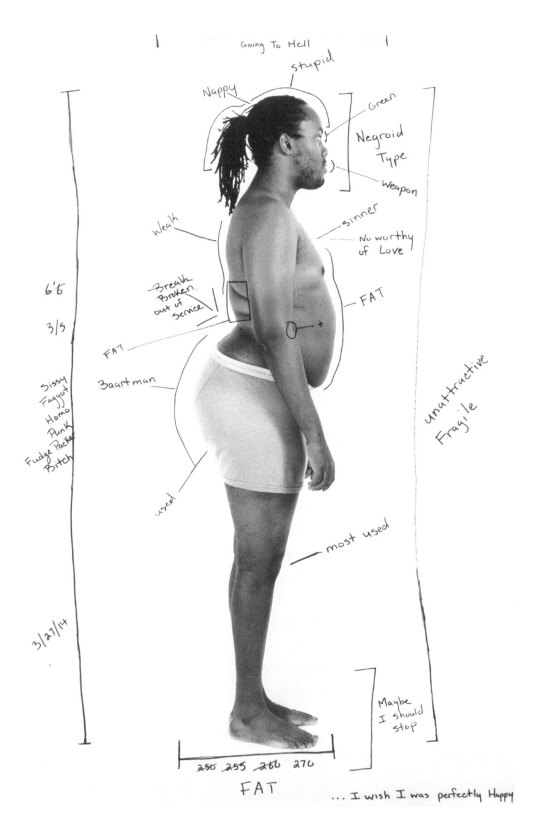

GLENN You moved to Oakland, California, from Triana, Alabama, at eighteen years old and have spoken about the pushback you received from family. What was it like saying goodbye, and did you have any fears or doubts about that move?

BRONTEZ Definitely! I think when you are young and embarking on a path that no one you know has gone through, there is so much fear. However, I remember crossing the state line with peace. When I first moved from Alabama, I actually tried to make it in Tennessee, so I stayed in Chattanooga for a bit. Then I moved to Indiana, and some friends in Southern Alabama were moving to Southern California, so I went from Indiana to California. I had a wobbly trajectory, but you have to be scared to be brave, and once it had sunk in that I was finally out of there, I felt a really tremendous amount of peace and I knew freedom was ahead of me. I never guessed it would eventually look like this, but I was pretty stoked.

G You've spoken about living a life of movement, one that mirrors the feeling you have while dancing. Do you find a need to pause, and if so, what does that look like?

B I think there is plenty of space for pause. The funny thing is it often looks like rapid-fire sessions. Putting out a decent book or record is a two-year process. I always manage my time, but I think in the beginning, I used to become extremely exhausted and burnout. I also couldn't rest too long because there was always something else to do. So I think you can, but it's easier to manage your time than you may think.

I always think about my cousins back in Alabama and one black girl in particular I used to work with. In 2006, I worked at Lush in the city; this was right before my artistic career really kicked off. So, this girl I worked with was a single mother of four kids, and she was also going back to college. She was just this awesome girl, and her hair was always in place, her eyelashes were always done. One day, I asked her, "How do you have four kids, go to school, and have a job?" She said, "If I sat down and thought about it, I wouldn't do it. I just do that shit." This woman had real responsibilities, and she was just getting shit done. When I go back to Alabama, some of my female cousins have two or three kids and they show up to the barbeque looking nice. I'm like, "If they can raise two or three kids by their goddamn selves, I can certainly put out a record. It's not that fucking hard."

There are so many people who work harder than me every day, and if I had those options, I would have a wealth of experience. Honestly, if it had been up to me, I would have just been a musician, playing in my white punk band for the rest of my life. But that scene was never going to uphold me in terms of representation politics. I was just too black, too queer, and too weird. I knew

I could get enough resources putting out records, but putting all of my eggs in one basket and having it fail would have been very disappointing for me. So I am glad because it forced me to explore different avenues in my creativity, and being here, living the artist lifestyle in warehouses, was a great way to explore different things at once.

You asked me about resting. I totally rest because everything is on a timer. It's kind of like when you have to cook a big meal for a bunch of people. You let the corn simmer while you are cutting up the carrots. Then, when the carrots are done, you check the roast.

G I want to talk about your work in "Me vs. The Writer" from *Johnny Would You Love Me If My Dick Were Bigger*. There's a line where you wrote, "Looking back, I think we were both jealous of each other." You go on to write about envying his success and even "wishing you were him." In a culture where we can literally scroll through hundreds of people's highlight reels in an app, how do you deal with jealousy? Is it something you encounter or deal with at all?

B Oh, yes, on so many levels. When I was a younger artist, I was definitely envious of other people's success, but in my twenties, I read this book by Sylvia Plath that talked about jealousy and not always taking it with you. She used a pretty good example in the book. Let's say you have a friend, and you both want to go to Europe. You want to go to France, but your friend wants to go to Italy. If your friend goes to Italy, you can't be jealous because that's not really want you wanted. No two people are really designed to have the same thing. This quote by Martha Graham is one of my go-tos: "Truly, the only person you are in competition with is yourself."

So with *Johnny Would You Love Me If My Dick Were Bigger,* there were a couple weird writer boys that I think were kind of jealous, but I'm pretty sure they came from a higher economic standing. That book was something that could have only been written by a working class boy because there was no real pedigree to protect in the world, no real consequences. If you have money and you write that book, you'll get written out of the will! I had a freedom to explore the extremes of what I wanted to talk about. So jealousy is funny, but more often than not, it isn't warranted. I think we all get accolades at different times. I've learned the hard way that not all of our fans show up at once.

YOU

TO

BE

TO

BE

HAVE
SCARED
BRAVE.

G In *Since I Laid My Burden Down*, the main character DeShawn has two past lovers, Arnold and Jattias, who committed suicide. Have you lost a loved one to suicide, or have you ever had suicidal proclivities yourself?

B Several. I have lost more friends to suicide than I even want to talk about. When we were partying and being crazy in our youth, it was just labeled as "wild." Then you get to a certain point where you are like, "Wait, some people are really just self-destructive." When we were young, I always thought it was something that would eventually work itself out or we would work it out of our system. That is not always the case, and sometimes you have to look at your patterns and ask yourself what you really want. I would have never called myself "suicidal," but I definitely engaged in self-destructive behavior. Going through that and seeing it gives you a new respect for life, a new lease on life. I always thought I was too sad, and I'd sit around and cry a lot because I wasn't rich enough or whatever. But when I look around and see how many of my friends did not make it, there is nothing else to do but express gratitude. I had to find outlets for my rage besides partying and drinking, and I had to find ways to get out of that negative, circular thinking.

G What advice would you give a young person who is working hard to manifest their dreams?

B Ninety-nine percent of any job is showing up, and that's the hardest fucking thing to do. The hardest part for me is not writing, it's typing. Genius is truly ninety-nine percent perspiration, one percent inspiration. If you wake up every day and do something, whether it's journaling or writing in huge spurts at a time, you will find success. But you have to consistently build on it until it's done. I'm an intense daydreamer, but that is how I work. I have to dream "big" into existence. I have to give myself time to think and execute. When it is time to execute, I actually have to execute. When I wrote *Since I Laid My Burden Down*, I was working as a waiter at The Castro and as a barber in this barbershop, still getting up and going to my college classes every day. During my waiting shifts, I wrote down everything that came to my head. I knew when I got home from school, I was not going to have the energy to do that shit. I eventually got a writing residency, but a big bulk of that book came from me writing on my breaks at work. It was worth it. After a year and a half, I had a book. It's a slow, arduous process, and there are all types of fucking potholes in the road. But I think if you stay the course and are really driven, it'll happen! Once you do it, once you know the process, it won't matter if it sucks, you'll just get it done because you always get better at your passion. That is what they don't tell you; you will always be better than you were before. It's really about showing up.

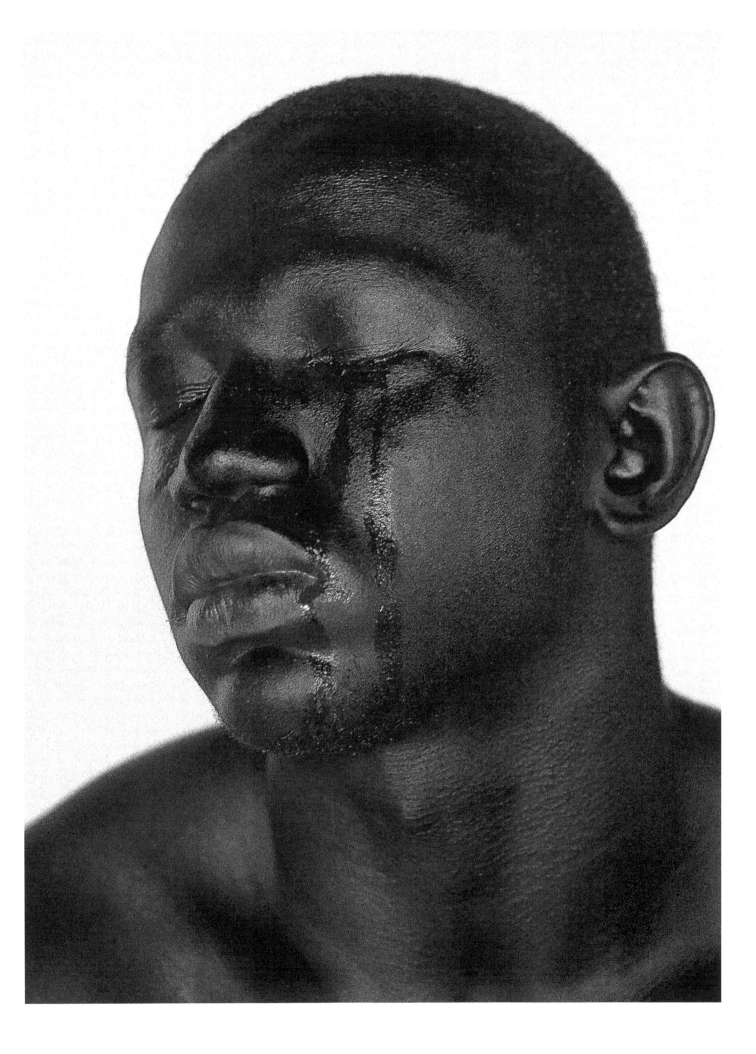

DOUGLAS

NEIL

REED

GLENN Black Men Heal's mission is to provide access to mental health treatment, psychoeducation, and community resources to men of color. Can you speak about how Black Men Heal does that?

DOUGLAS Well, like you said, one of our main goals is to offer free services to men of color. When COVID-19 started, we began offering free therapy sessions to men of color to aid in ending the stigma of mental health, and we have therapists who volunteer their time for these services. In our community, going to therapy is often seen as something "crazy people" do, and that's been our scapegoat. Now, with mental health especially, we can begin to go more in depth about how "crazy" may manifest in everyday life.

G There's a lot of pressure for black men to "be tough," and there's a pervading myth that opening up and being vulnerable is a sign of weakness. Why do you believe it's important for black men to open up about stressors, such as racism, economic disparities, or the traumas they've experienced?

D When you open up in a spiritual sense, you become free. Trying to be tough all the time is hard work. Trying to be something you are not and keeping that mask on is exhausting. When you're able to release that and be comfortable with yourself, you become liberated. I'm a man who grew up learning those things, and those philosophies mean nothing to me now because I'm able turn into Jeremiah the Prophet and shed a tear whenever my spirit moves me to. Those tears are a release of freedom. It puts you in a vulnerable yet safe place.

G Have you encountered men in the program who have a difficult time opening up? How do you address that and encourage them to express themselves?

D We state from the beginning that it's a free space. Men don't encourage each other enough, so being honest and saying it's an open environment and encouraging others to uphold that has helped. We started King's Corner when COVID-19 hit, and it's been amazing! We had a gentleman who was recently deployed, and he opened up about what was going on with him mentally. We had a guy whose friend just committed suicide, so we offered an open space to share our personal testimonies and uplift him. Our sincerity, passion, and honesty makes them feel us because we all have our own personal struggles, which sometimes makes us hesitant to share what is going on, but brother, these last few weeks have been amazing, and I'm the type of person who's realized that life is full of teachable moments. This conversation right here is a teachable moment.

G How did you initially get involved with Black Men Heal?

D Another board member called me and said, "Hey, Doug. I think you would be excellent as a board member in the organization. I told Tasnim, one of the founders, to reach out to you, get your background, and ask if you could become a board member." So they called me and gave me the spiel, and I told them, "I'm not the board member type. I'm an on-the-ground kind of guy, and I have a heart for men, especially black men. I've been through a lot, from being divorced to being broke to being homeless, so if you are looking for a boots-on-the-ground type of guy, I'm in."

G You worked as a correctional officer, and you've given lectures about correctional systems and prison reform at various organizations, including Columbia University. Can you speak about the parts of prison reform you're passionate about? What progress and hurdles have you seen while doing this work?

D I started working at the county jail in 1990 and retired in 2016. I came out of the military with a law enforcement frame of mind at the height of the 1986 anti-drug abuse act, so prisons were being built all over the country at rapid rates. I made the determination that I wasn't going to be unemployed for a long time, so I decided to work at the county prison. With that correctional officer position, I was able to see what was going on within the system. I had some knowledge of it, but I'd never actually seen what was going on and how it impacted people.

While I worked in receiving and discharging, I was in charge of processing the guys coming in and out of the institution. After they got off the bus, I had to strip-search them and pretty much violate them. It's the process, and after a while, I became immune to it. When I released guys, some would have family support, with their loved ones waiting outside with a limo. There were other guys who had just done like ten or more years, and they were scared. They didn't know what they were going to do. I always kept them in my mind because in prison, it was mostly *us*.

I made some adjustments while working in the prison, but it's a dangerous place. It's like being in your neighborhood; you may not know everybody by name, but you know their face. There was a level of comfortability working in that environment because, for the most part, everybody was black. There were blue coats and white guys who tried to treat the brothers poorly, but I wouldn't let it happen on my watch. Still, it was going on. After years of seeing that, I retired and began researching what was really happening behind the scenes. My foundation has always been my mother, and she was the kind of person who would take anybody in from off the streets. I really began evaluating the process, and I wanted to make a difference. I decided to start my own nonprofit called Synergy Reform.

MARK FLEURIDOR

Pg. 218
Adventures of Mako #1, 2020
© Mark Fleuridor.
Courtesy of the artist

WHEN YOU <u>OPEN UP</u> IN A SPIRITUAL SENSE, YOU BECOME <u>FREE.</u> TRYING TO BE TOUGH ALL THE TIME IS HARD WORK. TRYING TO BE SOMETHING YOU ARE NOT AND KEEPING THAT MASK ON IS <u>EXHAUSTING.</u> WHEN YOU'RE ABLE TO RELEASE THAT AND BE COMFORTABLE WITH YOURSELF, YOU BECOME <u>LIBERATED.</u>

TYLER MITCHELL

Pg. 222-223
Dazed Magazine:
In My Pink Polo, 2016
© Tyler Mitchell.
Courtesy of the artist

What turned the table for Synergy Reform was when Van Jones created the Redemption Project. The Redemption Project was an event which brought together criminals and violent crime survivors for an eye-to-eye talk to heal traumas and reform the criminal justice system. One of Van's associates, Sue Ellen Allen, whom I met in Seattle, is a big reason I was able to establish my platform and speak around the country.

I met Sue after the discussions and told her I was interested in starting a nonprofit organization. She gave me her card and told me if I called every Friday, she would assist me in creating my program. I called her for a few Fridays, and within a month, she invited me to Arizona to see exactly what her organization, Reinventing Reentry, was doing. Their aim is to help felons reenter society by helping them find work and assisting them with transportation needs, be it getting to the courthouse or meeting with their probation officer. Since I had worked in the prison system receiving and discharging inmates, I was able to add another element to what Reinventing Reentry was already doing.

I ended up going on tour with her, from New York to Tennessee, pleading our case of criminal justice reform to various legislators and educators.

G Have you dealt with depression, anxiety, PTSD, or other mental health issues while doing this work, and if so, how do you personally manage that stress?

D I can definitely relate with PTSD, having worked in the prison system for so many years. I kept asking myself, *Why are all the brothers in this institution black?* Black men get sentenced with way more time than white men for the same crime. It's crazy. I wouldn't say I've dealt with depression because I was able to bounce back, but I think a lot of those stressors contributed to me cheating on my wife, which ultimately led to our divorce. It also contributed to my money addiction, where my excessive overtime caused me to neglect my family and my kids. Dealing with racism on top of it all is tough. The most frustrating thing is that, oftentimes, you can't legally prove racism. I'm confident in the work I'm involved in though, and I'm growing everyday.

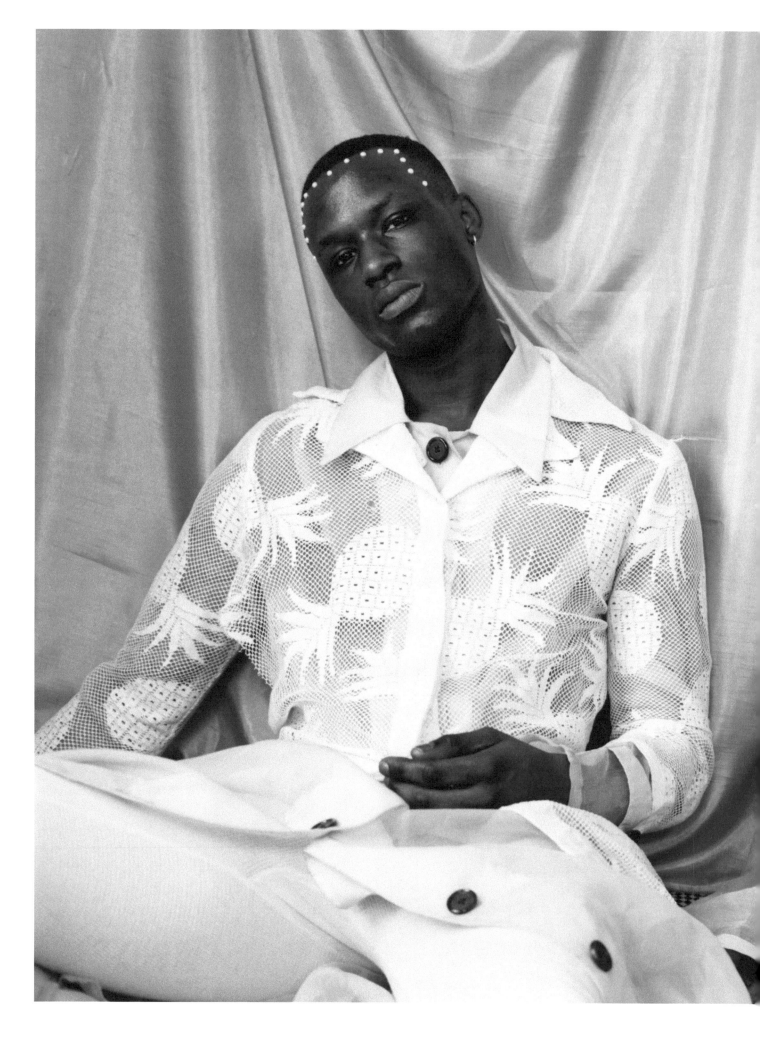

CAR

MAURICE

LOS

RUFFIN

AT AGE TWENTY-SEVEN,
I FELT LIKE A TOTAL FAILURE BECAUSE
I HADN'T PUBLISHED ANYTHING
I WANTED TO PUBLISH YET. I HAD RUN
OUT OF

HOPE

BY THAT POINT, BUT I HADN'T
RUN OUT OF

FAITH.

GLENN You were born and raised in New Orleans and were there when Hurricane Katrina hit. You've talked publicly about losing your home, as well as your neighborhood and the things that couldn't be replaced, like family photos. Can you speak about where you and your family were emotionally during that time and the rebuilding phase afterward? How did you get through it?

MAURICE In my household (my wife and I), we felt a sense of attachment to the community. We didn't want to live anywhere else. We considered not coming back because we were displaced for a while, but then, we were like, "Nah, this is home." Maybe at some point in the future we'll live somewhere else, but we can't be pushed out. Once we decided to come back and rebuild the house, there were no questions in our mind. I think that gave us purpose that helped us feel stronger than we had felt in the days before we knew what was going to happen. There was a time when the city was flooded, and it felt like it was going to stay flooded forever. We came together and worked, and that helped a lot, but I also don't want to erase the sadness.

Also, federal aid was lacking. That's the continuation of a story that's played out anytime a majority black community has been devastated. Now everybody's talking about Tulsa and how they were basically burned to the ground, and there's many other black communities during the Reconstruction era that were obliterated. I think New Orleans is kind of like the pandemic. Around March and April, people were really worried about the pandemic and recognized that black folks were being affected by it the most. During Katrina, it was the same situation. In our family, we decided to use our own resources and, frankly, take some risks. We eventually received a loan, but it wasn't a great situation, and it took a lot of struggle to get that money. I know a lot of other black folks couldn't get their hands on that money. We have two lawyers in our household, and it still took a lot of effort to get it.

G In addition to being a lawyer, you also worked as a restaurateur while earning your MFA (Master of Fine Arts). Can you speak about balancing all of those things, specifically while writing *We Cast a Shadow*, and what that looked like on a day-to-day basis?

M Sure, just to be clear, I had just finished my MFA when I opened the restaurant, but I was writing the book for sure. What I learned is if you're doing something that is important to you and you think it's going to be a gift to your community in some way, it becomes a lot less onerous to do it. I really felt like my community created me to be a writer, and it wanted me to tell some of our stories. So even though I was tired after a long day, it was OK. I still took thirty minutes to get a few pages down before I went to sleep. I definitely think the mission and connectedness to my people helped me get through it.

G Your debut novel *We Cast a Shadow* took four years to write and was released last year when you were forty-one years old. You also made a comment during a conversation with Kiese Laymon that "you could've turned it in after two years, but a voice told you to keep going." We live in a culture that is obsessed with the finished result and "the win" rather than the process. Can you speak about patience, the process, and if there was ever any anxiety or unhealthy yearning to be finished?

M There was definitely a feeling along the way that I needed to be done as soon as possible, but I would get to the end, look back, and it wasn't what I wanted it to be, so I had to start a new draft. The patience came from a sense of "this is not a hobby," and I'm not trying to crank it out fast. I want to create a beautiful work of art I'll be proud of once it gets into the world. I knew from experience that people who rushed their projects or allowed them to be influenced by other people's timelines were unhappy, and I can tell you now a year after my release, I feel perfectly satisfied with what I created. As a matter of fact, it exceeded my expectations.

G Looking at your life, I think there's a lot that can be learned about patience and things coming into fruition in its time. There are so many people who want to do that thing that's been on their heart for a long time and create that thing they want to share with the world. Going through your twenties and thirties, was there ever a feeling of "Is this going to happen?" or "When is this going to happen?" or did you trust the process, even earlier in your life?

M Yes, definitely. At age twenty-seven, I felt like a total failure because I hadn't published anything I wanted to publish yet. I had run out of hope by that point, but I hadn't run out of faith. I think the faith kept me on the path long enough to meet the people who became my writing family, and repeatedly, they inspired me to continue and not give up. I recognized that it really was an issue of sticking with it, and the longer I stuck with it, the more I accomplished my goals. That's been the case so far, and I believe that'll be the case going forward. Just stick with it, and it'll get done.

SEATON

ITH

GLENN You had a passion for comedy at a really young age and have spoken about growing up in the church. Your mother was a reverend, and you even served as a youth director. Growing up in a religious household, was there ever guilt attached to the entertainment you liked or your goal of being a stand-up comedian?

SEATON No, my mother went to a new-age church called Unity, and she became a reverend later in life, around forty years old. Her whole thing was "Everything is God" versus looking at the Bible in a literal sense. She actually put me onto Richard Pryor. Her and my grandmother had his albums, and she fostered my love for comedy.

Even when I was a youth director, it wasn't about religion. I worked at YOU Camp (Youth of Unity), which really was a camp for young kids who needed a hug. They felt odd and weird and crazy. I remember I used to say, "I'm not like these kids," but looking back, I was just like those kids! I didn't really understand the world, and I didn't know how to create love within myself. We learned the basic rules of life that, in retrospect, I'm really grateful for.

It's interesting because when we get really stressed, we revert from an adult to an insecure teenager to a child again. In those times, you have to go back to the tools you've picked up in life. Sometimes I'd get mad at my parents, but now, I look back like, "Yeah, they gave me some good tools." My mother used to say, "There's nothing lost in spirit," and I used to be so annoyed by that statement. Now, as an adult, I've realized you'll find whatever you're looking for. You really speak everything into existence. If you say, "Everything is lost," then everything will be lost.

G You graduated from Howard University and have spoken a bit about being called an "Oreo" by classmates because you listened to bands, like The Rolling Stones and The Beatles. You even mentioned that part of your decision to go to Howard was to find your blackness in some ways. Do you remember that time in your life, and when did you begin to understand yourself a bit more?

S I think I always knew who I was, but it was a matter of me accepting it. Growing up, my mother would move every couple of years, so I had already lived in California, Missouri, New Jersey, and North Carolina by the time I turned nine. I had seen everybody, but I didn't have the chance to act like everybody because I wasn't around anybody long enough. By the time I was a teenager, I didn't know how to act like anybody else. I just had anxiety. I thought maybe I wasn't black enough, so I moved to Washington D.C., went to Howard, and met other black people just like me. I realized I had to like me, then the people who liked me would be around me, and that would be my tribe.

G You joke about drinking and drugs in your stand-up, and I know when working in clubs, it's always around. Is drinking a big part of your life?

S Yeah, I definitely drink and smoke. Making jokes about cocaine is funny to me, but I've never done it. I just know I wouldn't stop. I'm always a little depressed or mad about things, but I'm constantly working on not being those things. So to know there's a drug that can take that burden away? Yeah, I wouldn't stop. I just have rules for myself.

G To follow up on that a little bit, what has depression looked like for you in your life, and have you been able to pinpoint the root of it?

S I think my depression was due to my lifestyle and a lack of understanding. During the times I felt really depressed, I didn't think I had control of my life, and in the moments where I forgot I had control of my life, my victimhood came up.

I'll say this: I'm suicidal, but it's not in the way most people think. When I was seven, I fell off a balcony, and I was told I died for a few moments. Ever since then, my perspective of death has been "Oh, that's what death is. That ain't shit." So in a way, I've looked at life as "Would I rather be here, or would I rather be dead?" Nine times out of ten, I'd rather be dead because this shit sucks! So that was the bad way I was thinking.

235

I found out when my mom had me, it broke up her first family. I'm not sure if she had an affair, but either way, she left her first family and got with my dad. Then, they broke up, and he ended up going out and having other families. So as a kid, I never felt like I had a place to fit in, and I unconsciously thought I was a mistake. I also moved around and didn't relate to other kids in school, and I never had a group unless it was the outcasts. Whenever I tried to fit in, I failed. So by the time I was nineteen, I was sick of life. At that point, I began to ask, "OK, what do I want to do for myself?" That's when I took control and began to do stand-up for real. I had done it for fun before, but I really began to take it seriously. I was like, "This is my choice in life" because I was sick of not having choices.

Here's one thing I discovered: We all act from our identity. So whenever I'm saying things to myself, like "Oh, I'm stuck" or "Nobody can help me," whatever that shitty statement is, you have to look at that voice and say, "Who would say something like that?" I realized someone who thought they were a mistake would say something like that. I didn't know that was my thought process, but now that I know, I can fix it.

In the Bible, it says "I Am," and those are the most powerful words you can say. If you say things, like "I am a blessing. I am great. I am a good person. I am loved. I am love," that's the key. Our brains create our reality. Things are never "happening;" it's more so how our brains are interpreting it.

There's a book called *Man's Search for Meaning* by Viktor Frankl. He was a psychiatrist who was captured and sent to a concentration camp. He survived the Holocaust and wrote this book about the attitudes of people who survived versus the attitudes of people who died. Most of the people who died were the ones who lost hope, and many of the people who lived were the ones who could find joy in the crumbs of a biscuit. They would keep finding those little moments of joy to live off of, and that's the most important thing.

I AM

ARE THE MOST POWERFUL WORDS YOU CAN SAY.

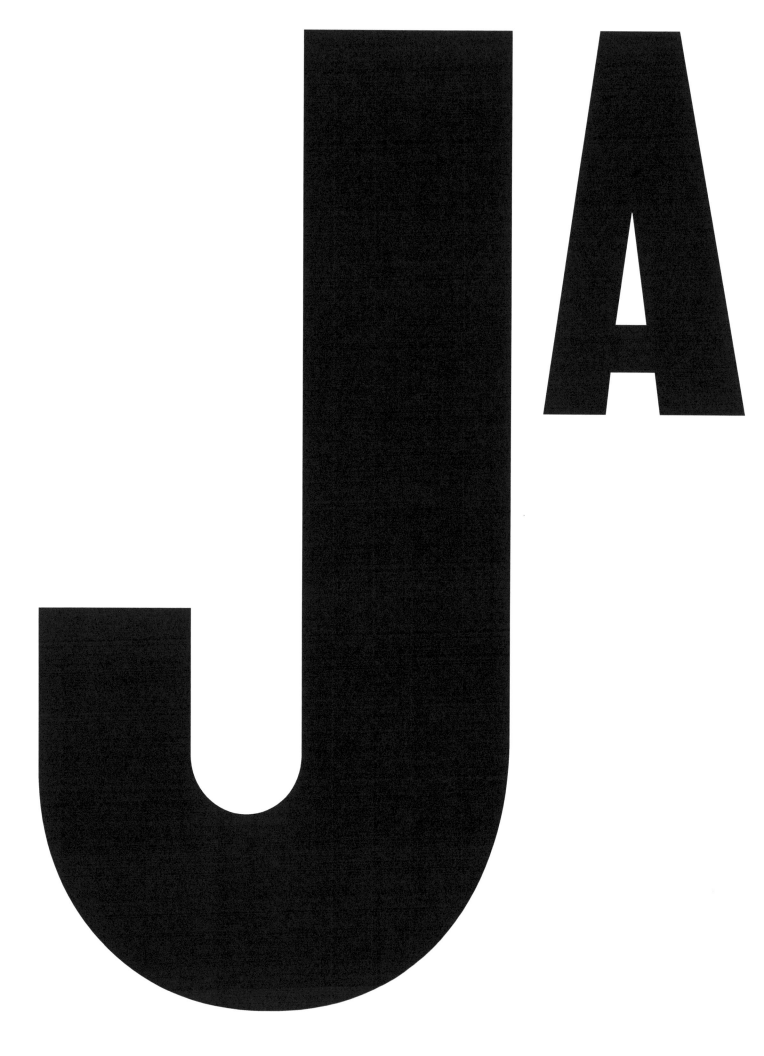

MES

SPOONER

GLENN I wanted to start by asking you about your film *Afro-Punk* that you directed almost twenty years ago. Do you remember when the idea for the film came and why you wanted to create it?

JAMES I was twenty-three, living in Williamsburg, Brooklyn, and hanging out in a white-dominated community. A lot of stuff was happening around me, and I went through that thing a lot of college kids go through where they are entering a new world and have that "aha" moment, I was learning about black identity and figuring out who I was.

When that moment hit, I started to look at the black people and other people of color in my friend circle and ask them some questions, like "Do we really connect with our given identity as much as our chosen identity?" I decided around that time to take a trip to St. Lucia, where my family is from.

I was hoping to go "back home," so to speak, on that trip. There is a part of me that always thought I didn't relate to the mainstream, hip-hop, gang-banging black kids, because I was Caribbean. So I thought that by going back to the island, I would find my people. But moments after I got off of the plane, I realized I didn't know anything about that either.

G What kind of questions spawned during that visit to St. Lucia, and what, if anything, led to the film?

J Well, I had this ridiculous idea that I would get off of the plane and people would be like, "Brother! Welcome!" I don't know exactly why I thought that. The reaction to my arrival was more like, "Oh, you are American. Give me money." Coupled with the fact that I'm light-skinned, my sibling who lived there always thought of me as their white brother.

I found out that, in St. Lucia at least, it doesn't matter that I am half-black. I am considered white because of my skin tone. That fucked me up. So I definitely was in a daze while in St. Lucia. I started locking my hair and had this reactionary response like, "Oh, I am going to show you how black I am." When I got back home, I did all of the reactionary shit. I broke up with my white girlfriend, I moved away from Williamsburg, moved into a black neighborhood, and I really just had this thought stuck in my mind, like "Fuck this shit." I had always thought of myself as black, and it turned out, I had been lying to myself all this time.

I was a sculptor at the time—or at least that's how I was expressing myself—and I decided to move out of my loft into a smaller space. I started thinking, *How can I tell the story of my identity struggle?* At the time, I was also really mad at the punk scene for equipping me with all of these progressive politics, but the conversation around race was limited to extremism. I wanted to keep the punk ideals, but I wanted to challenge the black mainstream and the white underground. I really was just angry, and I wanted everyone to pay, and the way I went about doing that was making the film.

G In your work, there seems to be a recurring theme of identities and examining the loneliness we face within them. Ironically, by exploring that, you've been able to create this communal aspect. Did you feel lonely growing up, either personally or emotionally?

J Loneliness? Yes and no. I moved a lot as a kid, so I became really good at making friends. It wasn't hard for me to move around different environments and become known within that scene, but there was a certain validation I was always looking for. When I first made *Afro-Punk,* I could literally name all the black people I knew outside of my family. They were basically all of the members of TV on the Radio. (laughs)

I was determined to be a part of the black community, whatever that meant. I went through a few moments of "OK, I like soul music, and I DJ soul music, but I do it with all of these white kids. Where are all of the black people that like this?" Thankfully, in New York, it was easy to find a variety of black scenes like that because there were Stevie Wonder parties and things like that. Within three or four months, I was throwing those parties with big DJs like Bobbito and Spinna.

I wouldn't say I was lonely in a bored or depressing way, but it was more like I worried that I wasn't authentically black. I felt that way until I completed *Afro-Punk* and started screening it. I had done eighty interviews, spent two years editing it and then hearing the stories of so many black people at the screenings was like going to therapy.

241

I finally realized I wasn't alone. I'll never forget going to the American Black Film Festival for my second screening of the film. I had two or three sold-out shows at this mainstream, bougie, black festival. These are people I would normally never spend time with. They were just mainstream, American black people who go to cookouts and church and watch football—normal folk. I remember thinking, *If these people were as interested in me as a kid as they were for the film, I never would have made it in the first place.* They all came to see this screening, and afterward, I was surrounded by so many people who could relate, whether they were the only black kid on the lacrosse team or the only black person at the office. They connected with me on this idea that sometimes they don't see themselves as authentically black because the idea of blackness is very narrow, especially when BET was in its prime. People tend to forget that Skateboard P (Pharrell Williams) wasn't a thing yet. Your only options were Puffy and Jay-Z or Erykah Badu and OutKast.

G What led you to turn this film into a festival?

J I had been screening the film relentlessly, whether it was at festivals, punk screenings, or DIY shows. I ultimately ended up showing over three hundred screenings in three years. So for the one-hundredth screening, I wanted to do some kind of celebration. There was a punk band at the time making noise in New York called Stiffed, and their lead singer was Santi White who went on to be Santigold. People were starting to know her, and she had just written an album for a singer named Res, so a lot of neo-soul girls were following her. I wanted her to play at my celebration, so I contacted her and she got me in touch with her manager Matthew Morgan, who eventually became my partner in Afro-Punk. We started planning monthly events together.

The message board was really starting to take off and long story short, in 2005 we decided, "Let's have an Afro-Punk Film Festival. We can show all of these radical black films, we could book bands and make it an Afro-Punk weekend." People from the message boards would fly in, and it was an opportunity for everyone to meet in person. For at least the first three years, I was the head booker, and from the lineups, you can see I was actively trying to create a new lane for black people.

After I left the company, the motivation for this new lane went away. So if you fast forward to the 2010 festival, the headliners were Lenny Kravitz and Grace Jones, which was big, then the next year was Erykah Badu. The focus became repackaging the mainstream as "punk" or alternative.

Ironically, I started AFROPUNK as an alternative to mainstream blackness, like BET and *Essence*, but now, the owner of *Essence* magazine owns AFROPUNK. If you think about the people who have headlined AFROPUNK in the past seven years, they have all headlined *Essence Festival*. Yesterday, someone sent me a screenshot from the AFROPUNK website that says they're hosting a book club featuring Daymond John from Shark Tank, and that he'll be reading a book to people. I literally thought it was a joke and someone was clowning! It felt like such an *Essence* thing to do, so I have all of these experiences that slowly pushed me away and culminated in me leaving what I created. It is just weird to see what it has become.

But also, there is a beautiful silver lining because there are all of these black and brown punk rock festivals that have started in reaction; they're doing their own thing, building a P.O.C. punk community.

G On your Instagram page, you've opened up about some of the hardships you faced growing up, writing about the impact of divorce, abuse, neglect, and chemical imbalances. Has exploring those topics in your work served as therapy, and/or have you found the need to speak about those things with a professional?

J I've definitely had therapy, and I would love to continue. Referring to the chemical imbalance post, I was talking about a kid I had recently met who experienced that. Fortunately, I haven't dealt with those issues. However, I have witnessed a lot of abuse. My dad beat my mom, he cheated, and it later came out that he was a pedophile. Thankfully, that behavior wasn't directed toward me. I had to be the go-to person for my siblings who were affected. I've witnessed a lot.

Ultimately, I don't think we have enough conversations about these things, certainly with young boys. When I was eighteen, I found this book titled *Surviving Masculinity* that discussed how the oppression of women affects men. I really attached myself to that book, telling myself I would never be that person who can't talk about sensitive subjects.

HOW CAN I TELL THE STORY OF MY IDENTITY STRUGGLE ?

OFOE AMEGAVIE

Pg. 244
12 o'clock in Accra, 2019
© Ofoe Amegavie.
Courtesy of the artist

As I get older, I see the ways I get defensive, shut down, or refuse to share my opinions. I'll listen to other people talk but won't say what's on my mind. I believe everyone has their issues that keep them from being able to love fully, and I'm working to crack those things open within me on a daily basis.

G I think there were a lot of false truths many of us grew up believing when it came to "what it means to be a man." In many ways, your work reminds me of certain conceptual artists, in that the projects themselves seem to come out of an idea you're examining. Is that how you approach these projects and films? For example, the monthly Freedom Ride: Black Kids On Bikes ride. How did that project start?

J Thank you for doing your research! Well, shortly after I moved to California, I was just coming off of Afro-Punk, and I got a job as a video producer. My girlfriend was using my car because she worked further than me, so I was biking to work. Something happened to it, and I needed to fix it, so I found this bike co-op. I ended up loving it, so I got into building bikes and was invited to go on a group ride. This ride was called Crank Mob and about three hundred people showed up. I looked around and saw there was only seven black people there; it was like a punk show!

I pulled one of the riders aside and asked why there weren't any black people on the ride. He said everyone was invited; they just have to come. I was like, "Oh, *that* old story." So I decided I wanted to make a ride for black people. After that, I made a routine of stopping by every bike shop to see what they had and to get the lay of the land. I came across a bike shop run by two black dudes, and the three of us started talking about a black ride called Freedom Ride. They thought it was dope, so we organized our first ride with about fifteen people. I made spoke cards calling it the Freedom Ride with the byline "Black Kids on Bikes," but everyone got attached to that byline. Eventually it became Black Kids on Bikes, aka Freedom Rides. We would do these rides once a month, and while I was organizing them, we handed out spoke cards every month with a different letter, so if you came every time, you could eventually spell "Freedom Ride" on your bike.

I think at the height of it, we had eighty people show up, and it started to become to hard to keep organized. We would ride to the Watts Towers and people would get excited and start honking their horns thinking we were doing some kind of protest when really we were just riding bikes.

They were surprised to see so many black people on bikes! When Michael Jackson died, we did a ride up to his house in Bel-Air. We ended up in an Armenia protest, and we started yelling, "Freedom, freedom!" and the crowd chanted it back! They were screaming for us; it was bananas. Everybody is trying to be free! There was a freak-out everywhere we went. We were doing the most benign thing; we may as well have been jumping rope, but going through Bel-Air, we had a police escort through the entire neighborhood. Thankfully, nothing bad ever happened. We would ride through black neighborhoods and other black people would follow on their bikes.

I eventually burned out and stopped organizing. The rides still happen, but less frequently. Again, it was about trying to find community and proving to myself that black people can do anything and that I'm not a weirdo for liking shit black people aren't supposed to like.

G What led you to becoming vegan?

J I got into veganism when I was sixteen through the Heartcore scene. It was one of those intersectional politics where I was asking, "How could I be a feminist? How could I be a champion for gay people and civil rights but eat meat?" I wanted to be as consistent as possible, so I got into veganism.

I realized there was even more to it when I became a tattoo artist. About eight months into tattooing, I realized there was all kinds of animal products I was working with. So I streamlined my work to match my politics, and all of a sudden, I found myself a part of another community. I never looked for vegans to hang out with, but once I announced that my tattooing was all vegan, my business quadrupled, going from having almost no clients to having clients every day. I met so many vegans, and it reinvigorated me. Again, being yourself and putting yourself out there creates community.

DARRYLL

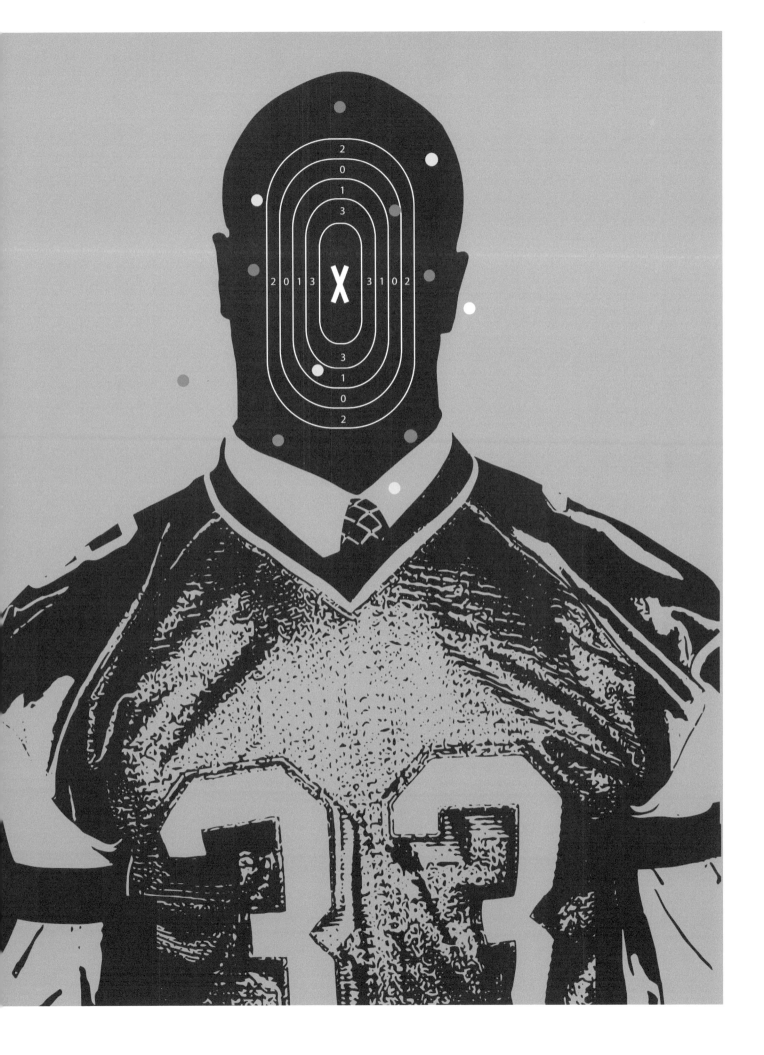

GLENN I came in contact with your work through your TEDx Talk "Overcoming Rejection," in which you discuss why and how rejection can serve as our friend rather than our enemy. You also opened up about the role football had in your life and how a pinched nerve in your back while playing Division I college football at Central Michigan University crushed your dream of playing in the NFL. You mentioned that there was a pressure to pull your family out of poverty. Was there this idea that you'd be the breadwinner that would take care of the entire family?

DARRYLL Yeah, I call it the Unspoken Honor Code, and it exists in a lot of minority communities. It's the idea that you feed the people who feed you. Growing up, my mom wasn't technically a single parent, but my father was off playing football, so she was carrying a lot of the weight. She was also taking care of two other kids whose father was absent. Even though my dad was doing a relatively good job helping out, their dad was gone, so she only had one father who paid child support and helped raise the children.

I watched my mom work two jobs and figure out a way to make it happen every year, whether it was buying shoes or new school clothes. I saw her put herself on the back burner to make our lives better, and as you get older, you think about the sacrifices your parents and grandparents made to make sure you have a better life. So when you get an opportunity, it's this unspoken rule that you're going to take care of them. My mom was never like, "Hey, when you make it, you better do something for me!," but there was definitely an unspoken idea that I wouldn't be who I am if they hadn't done what they did.

G In that TEDx Talk, you also revealed that once you had come to terms with your career-ending back injury, you fell into a deep depression and became suicidal. You've stated that you would drive while intoxicated, you would try to take your life by overdosing on pills, and at one point, you attempted suicide by means of starvation. Would you be willing to share some of the thoughts that were going through your head at that time and what depression looked and felt like for you?

D Yeah, I think it stemmed from everyone relating to me because of my success as an athlete. It was how everyone viewed me, and without that, I began to wonder if I mattered. At the same time, I thought nothing would fulfill me like being an athlete did. I really enjoyed playing football, and I thought I would never enjoy any other career path besides being a professional athlete. It's hard to describe those feelings, but the thought of what my life was going to be was a dreadful thought. The future didn't look as bright as the past, and I was like, "What's the point of the future if it's just downhill from here?"

That mindset is what really began to drive those depressive thoughts, as well as the fact that I was alone. The people who used to come around and ask how my family was doing were no longer there, and that really validated that insecurity, like "See, I knew I didn't matter. I only mattered because I was good at sports, and now that I'm unable to play anymore, no one cares about me."

On top of that, I had a girlfriend I had been dating for over four years, who, when I stopped playing, left me for another man. I remember thinking she wouldn't have left me if I was still going to the NFL. So it was a mixture of all of those thoughts —football's gone, she's gone, my friends are gone—and all of that pushed me to that point.

G After your final suicide attempt, you were admitted to the psychiatric unit at Henry Ford Hospital in Detroit, Michigan, and it was there that you had what you've described as a life-changing experience. You've said it was there that you came to believe that your life still mattered, which led to you reading books about purpose, praying, and adopting a meditation practice that has ultimately shaped you into the man you are today. What happened while you were in that unit that had such a profound impact on your mindset and ultimately changed your life?

D When I went to Henry Ford Hospital, I was agnostic, and while I was there, two different women at two different times told me I needed to say yes to God. It was this supernatural encounter with two different people saying the exact same thing, and I knew it must've been God's way of working through people to reach me, and that gave me the strength to keep going. I felt that if God cared about me while I was selling drugs, contemplating suicide, and not even believing in Him, there must be a reason I'm alive and a purpose for me outside of sports.

ADRIAN A. FRANKS

Pg. 248-249
10 Shots for Help, 2013
© Adrian A. Frank.
Courtesy of the artist and
Museum of
Contemporary African
Diasporan Arts (MoCADA)

Since I was agnostic before that encounter, I still had a lot of questions. I wanted to know where the Bible came from and if it was really a white man's religion. I investigated all of the things I was taught about Christianity. I went on this journey and began to study and research the Bible and began asking, *What's my purpose? Is there something that will fulfill me more than sports?*

G In addition to your public speaking engagements, you're a pastor and a married man with three young daughters. You're also the founder of Second Chance Athletes, which you've described as holistic athletic transition services for current and former athletes. Can you speak about that organization, the work you're doing there, and the impact you're seeing in your clients' lives?

D After I left the psychiatric unit, I spent about five years reading, praying, and learning about myself through self-reflection and meditation. I came to this place where I realized that if I was offered a professional athletic contract, I wouldn't take it because I loved my life at that time more than I had loved my athletic life. I noticed my peers didn't feel the same way. They had careers, and some even had careers they were passionate about, but they still wished they could be playing sports, and I didn't. I began reflecting on how I had come to that place, and I saw that there were five specific phases I had gone through: accept, believe, discover, perceive, and persist, and that became our transition roadmap. I started walking athletes through the five phases of transition that helped me go from suicide to success, and now we're in the process of licensing that program and broadening the scope to help people transition from other aspects of life, such as being an active duty soldier.

G During that dark patch of your life, were you diagnosed with clinical depression, and is it something you take medication for and/or still wrestle with at times?

D I was diagnosed with clinical depression before that moment in my life, but it wasn't something I really dealt with because sports had been an outlet for me. Once that happened, I was forced to face my depression, fears, and insecurities, and I started to take my mental health very seriously. I began going to psychologists and counselors and learning how to live with depression. That's also when I started taking antidepressants, and I still take them to this day to maintain a healthy chemical balance. I also make sure I maintain healthy habits. I journal every day, pray every day, reflect on the day, eat whole foods and take time to do nothing. It's still something I deal with, but medication and the practices I've put in place make it easier to manage.

I JOURNAL
DAY, PRAY
REFLECT ON
WHOLE FOOD
TIME TO

EVERY.

EVERY DAY,

THE DAY, EAT

S AND TAKE

DO NOTHING.

TIMOTHY SHORT

*A Dark in the Light
(You Are All
You Need)*, 2020
© Timothy Short.
Courtesy of the artist

RYANT

TERRY

An Attack Against One
Is An Attack Against All

The Slaughter of Black
People Must Be Stopped!
By Any Means Necessary!

Distributed by The Robert Brown Elliott League, 540 McAllister Street, San Francisco, Calif.

Pg. 258
Black Panther Party poster:
*An Attack Against One Is An
Attack Against All. The Slaughter
of Black People Must Be Stopped!
By Any Means Necessary!*
Distributed by the Robert Brown
Elliott League, c. 1968-69.
Courtesy of The Merrill C. Berman
Collection

GLENN I wanted to start by asking you about your work as a food justice activist. You founded b-healthy! in New York, a nonprofit that educates young people about food politics and introduces ideas on how to bring nutritious foods into their communities. Now, you serve as the chef-in-residence at the Museum of the African Diaspora (MoAD) in San Francisco. There, you're creating public programming at "the intersection of food, farming, health, activism, art, culture, and the African Diaspora." Can you speak about why that work is so important to you and how food justice activism manifests through your work with MoAD?

BRYANT I think I should start by saying that my work is grounded in grassroots food just as much as activism. Everything I have done—writing books, media, etc.—came after the work I was doing since 2000. I think the big things for me was, one, understanding the larger public health crisis we are facing, and two, recognizing the exponential rise in illnesses over the past thirty to forty years. I think I was mostly bothered by the fact that most young people were getting caught in the crosshairs of multi-national corporations that are more concerned about increasing their profits than public health or the environment. So when I learned about things like type 2 diabetes affecting more young people (early onset diabetes) than ever before, I knew something had to be done.

When I think about the reality so many young people face in terms of school lunch options, I realize how it's not even really food. As Michael Pollen would say, "It's just edible, food-like substances." When I think about the reality of young people in this country and the very few resources they have in their neighborhood to get healthy, fresh, affordable, and safe food, I'm moved to do this work because I feel like we need to do better for the young people. In my mind, our job is to create a better world for subsequent generations, so when I think about some of the most powerful movements in the twenty-first century, from the apartheid movement in Africa to the civil rights movement in the US, I realize it was often young people on the front lines. Their brilliance, bravery, and willingness to put it all on the line is incredible.

For the social justice movement to be successful, we have to train a generation of young people to take the lead. The young people who are living in the communities most impacted by food insecurities should be the ones leading and driving the change. They are most intimately connected to the intricacies of those communities and situations, and oftentimes, I think they have brilliant ideas on how to overcome them. These communities need resources and power shifted to them so they can be autonomous and self-determined to make a change.

When we talk about food issues, we shouldn't look at food in a vacuum. So much intersects with the food system, so for me, we can't just talk about bringing food to these communities. I often say that most food-insecure communities have very little access to fresh, safe, affordable, culturally appropriate foods. These are the same communities that have crumbling infrastructures, underfunded public schools, and very little green space to be active. Oftentimes, these people are also dealing with environmental racism. There are factories and industries in these communities that impact the health of the people living there. So I feel like food is a great way to start the conversation, and it has the ability to pivot to a number of different issues, like human rights and labor issues. Food is a great avenue for me to talk about the issues I think we should all be focusing on.

G You've opened up on social media about engaging in prison abolition while in New York City during the late '90s, and you've even facilitated giveaways to bring awareness and funding to Critical Resistance, a group dedicated to eradicating imprisonment while creating long-term alternatives to incarceration. Can you speak about that time in your life, the work you were doing in that space, and what it was like to do that work at that time?

B When I was living in New York, I wasn't necessarily working in a nonprofit that was trying to dismantle the prison industrial complex. What happened was, around '99, my ex-girlfriend and I read an article in *Vibe Magazine* about these two brothers. I think they attended Howard University, and they were twins. One of them or maybe both of them had gotten caught up in some drug conspiracy. Guilty or not, they were found to be guilty and were sentenced to ten years in prison. This was the first sentence they had ever had; they no record up until that point, and there were a lot of questions and doubts surrounding their involvement in the conspiracy they were implicated for. So we started doing research about the prison industrial complex. We started throwing fundraisers to send money to the legal funds of the young men we had read about. I think we did maybe three or four of them, but this was around the time my ex-girlfriend and I were into drum and bass. We did these live drum and bass shows, and we had a lot of connections in the art community in NYC. We curated the shows, and we would get live musicians, singers, and poets to perform. Then we would have these dope live drum and bass bands playing with people spittin' their rhymes and poetry. That was my first experience with that particular issue.

Then, my next girlfriend was working for this organization called Drug Policy Alliance, and they've been the leader in the push for decriminalizing drugs and rebelling against the failed war on drugs. Being with her and building a community of folks in that network, I learned even more about the foundation of the prison industrial complex and how the criminalization of drugs decimated black communities. So this has just been one of those constant touch points in my life that kept me aware of the way our so-called "justice system" is failing people, particularly its design to continuously oppress, marginalize, and imprison black folks. It's an issue I feel very deeply about. Now we've reached a new moment in which privileged white people and corporations are striving to make millions of dollars off this plant that has resulted in so many brothers being locked up for decades. When I was invited onto the show *Bon Appetite* on VICE Network, I told them I would do it on the condition that they let me talk about the prison industrial complex and the impact marijuana criminalization has had on black communities. They were cool and excited about it, so I went on there and talked about it. But of course they edited my five-minute talk down to like five seconds or something. I had re-read Michelle Alexander's *New Jim Crow* like three times, and I had my shit on point. They edited it, but I just continue on.

I have been a supporter of Critical Resistance over the years, but especially in this moment when we are having more open conversations about the need to abolish the police force. Unfortunately, there is no room for reform; we have played that game for far too long, and we need to defund it. In some cases, I believe we need to abolish police and look at other models for keeping our neighborhoods safe because clearly this isn't working for all of us. It was never really meant to work for us, as we have seen in the '60s with the founding of the Black Panther Party. They addressed the same issues we are dealing with now, so fast forward to 2020, clearly this is not working.

G Your fifth and most recent book, *Vegetable Kingdom*, is a cookbook with many plant-based recipes rooted in African traditions. During the book tour, you chatted with Tiffani Patton of Real Food Media. You opened up about taking a six-year break between the publishing of *Afro-Vegan* and *Vegetable Kingdom*, and said, "The cookbook writing process is isolating, protracted, and grueling. It's not fun at all." Can you speak about the realities of writing this book, the day-to-day process of it, and how you remained in the space you needed to be in as a father and husband?

HONOR TITUS

Pg. 261
Il Posto, 2019
© Honor Titus.
Courtesy of the artist
and Timothy Taylor,
London / New York

B That's a great question. You know, over the years, I've started thinking about the idea of work/family balance, but that reality just doesn't work for me. It may work for some people, but I think, as a creative person, I don't work a nine-to-five where you just check in and out of work. Sometimes being productive may not look like me sitting in front of a computer and typing words. It may just be me sitting there and doing nothing or being idle so I can be open to Infinite Intelligence, The Universal Mind, God, The Creator, Spirit or whatever you choose to call it. There is an entire force moving through me because I know so many of my ideas are not necessarily mine. They are things others have said and I have added to. I recognize that the work I am doing is often standing on the shoulders of many ancestors and elders who came before me; this is nothing new. This is just a different historical moment, and I am trying to make sense of it.

Writing is a deeply spiritual process, and I feel like I am connecting to my ancestors, an intelligence I can use to produce my best work. My meditation and prayer practice are things I feel like are inextricably linked to writing a book. I will say this, in the past, when I was doing book one and two, I would rely heavily on cannabis. I love cannabis. I understand the way it can open you up and lubricate your creativity. I found that was almost a replacement for the spiritual work I do in grounding myself and connecting to Source. I feel like my spiritual work and meditation allows me to go deeper and connect in a different way and I'm able to tap into information and energy I wouldn't be able to tap into otherwise.

We built a work shed for me in the backyard, which serves as my creative space. It is the place where I find comfort. I can attempt to replicate what I used to do before we had kids, when I was working for days on end without coming up for air. During those times, I could really sink deep into the creative process. My only responsibility was the work, so it is a bit different now that I have a wife, children, and many other responsibilities. Part of the reason for my hiatus was because I had been so immersed in writing and promoting *Afro-Vegan* that I felt like I missed my family, and I wanted to be a central part in their lives early on. I want to be a great model and create values for them to get them started on the right foot. I have so much pride, and I think I might have mentioned this in that interview with Tiffani, but I take so much pride in the fact that I took my daughter to

every single cello lesson up until I started working on a new book. I feel like that time is invaluable, and you can't get those years back. Having that gap allowed me to be with my family and feel good about going into another book phase. If I can focus on the work, I know it can be the best product. I am just thankful that my wife and family have been supportive and have given me that space. As much as they may miss me, when I am working on a book like *Vegetable Kingdom*, I miss weekends, holidays, and family trips, but I felt like I needed to be writing. In the moment, it is really challenging for them, but when they have the book in hand, I think they understand the sacrifice and how it can offer a gift to the world.

G I wanted to ask about a post you shared on Instagram in which you posted one of Octavia Butler's journal entries that listed concrete visions she saw for herself, including "being a best-selling author, being read by millions of people, and buying a beautiful home in a great neighborhood." You wrote that you came across it on the day you found out several goals you'd been praying about and meditating on for two years had manifested. You wrote, "I have entries in my journal from twenty years ago similar to this one where I mapped out many of the things that have come to fruition in my life. You have to put the work in, but defining your major purpose in life and writing down your goals are the first steps toward manifesting your desires." Can you speak about prayer and meditation, the role they serve in your life, and what those practices look like for you?

B Well, first of all, I will say my understanding of metaphysics and manifesting has helped my destiny unfold. That came from a lot of reading and studying in college, and I ran across a number of prominent writers and self-help gurus. Napoleon Hill's *Think & Grow Rich* has been one of the most vital books in terms of me being self-determined and controlling my destiny. I try to map out my life as much as I can, but I know there always has to be room for spirit to guide you to a place you might not know of, a place you need to go to. Instead of being dead set on "This is success" and "This is how the completion of this goal should look," I was clear on the direction I wanted to go in, but I was open to how it might look different than what I originally imagined. Hill's book is so rich with information and practices to help people move toward success. When you see the title, you think it is some get-rich-quick book, but as an author, I understand the ways publishers think in terms of marketing. I say that because oftentimes people think books like those are written by snake oil sales people, and to be fair, those people are out there. But I have studied people like Napoleon Hill, Catherine Ponder, and Andrew Carnegie with *How to Win Friends*. I have put in a lot of work; it is not just some willy-nilly stuff, so that work has allowed me to develop maintainable habits and practices.

I KNOW THERE IS A LOT OF <u>FUCKED-UP</u> STUFF HAPPENING AROUND THE WORLD, BUT THERE'S A LOT OF JOY AS WELL, PARTICULARLY IN MY OWN LIFE. I WANT TO <u>FOCUS</u> ON THE <u>GOOD THINGS</u> SO I AM ABLE TO CONFRONT THE INJUSTICES HAPPENING IN THE WORLD.

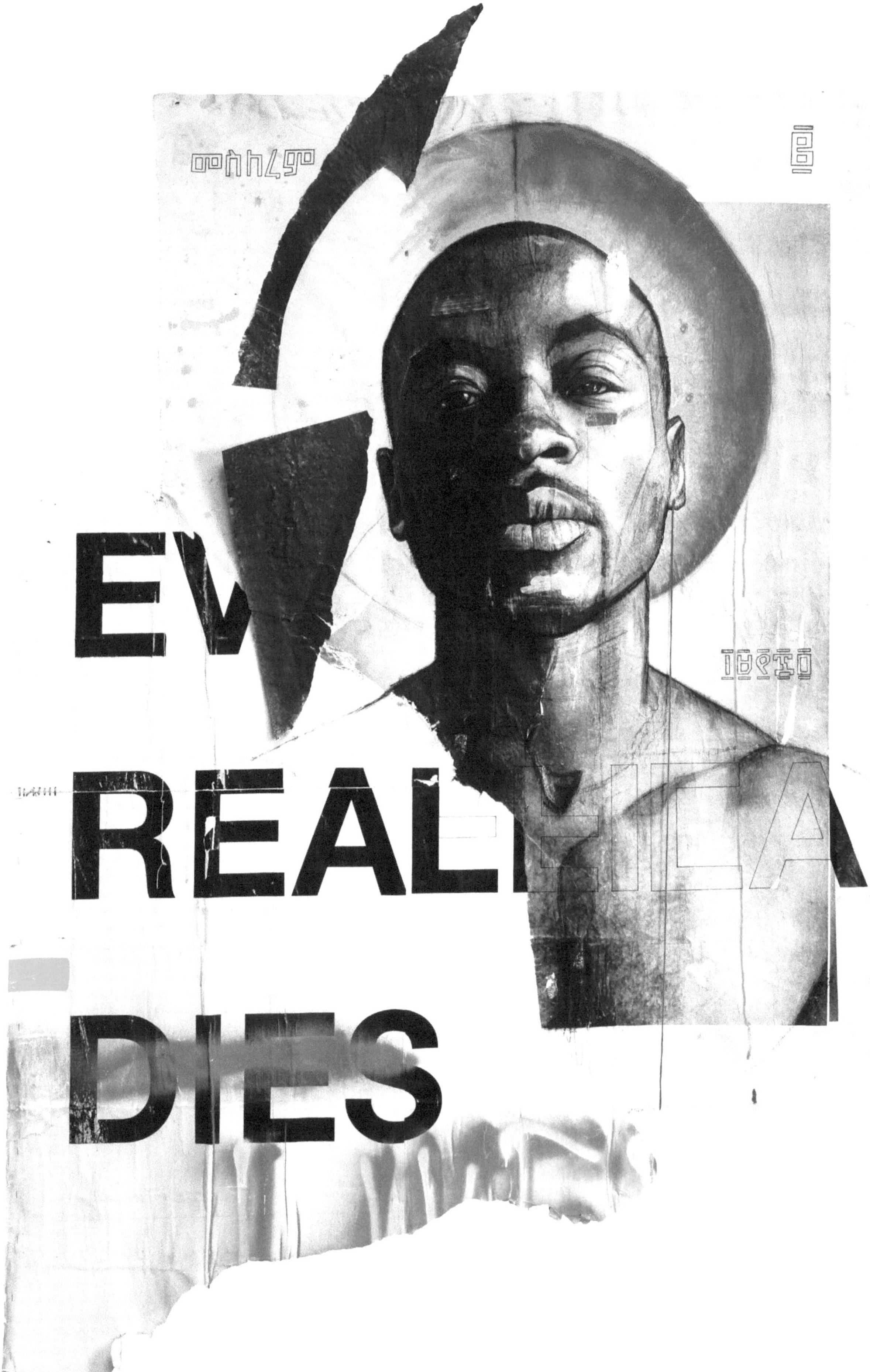
EV
REAL
DIES

Sometimes I forget those years where I was going to workshops and learning how to do these different practices, failing, succeeding, and starting over again. Now, I feel like I am in a rhythm. Part of it is that I have demonstrated in my own life how powerful things are and how successful I can be when I put the work in. I have done the work and put the labor into it for so long, and I see the outcomes manifest. Now, it's not a matter of if, but when. Whatever I want, I feel like I can have. If I have a goal I want to achieve, I put it out there, take actionable steps, and create long-term and short-term goals. If I can't get it, then that means I don't need to have it.

So in terms of daily practices, when I get up, I strive to do this, but I am not going to say I do it every day because every day is different, especially in this moment. However, I usually take care of my altars to my blood ancestors and spiritual ancestors. I have three altars for Edna Lewis, who is this giant in the food world and one of my inspirations. I talk to them and give them water, fruit, tea, or whatever. Then, I do my morning stretches and push-ups to get my heart pumping, and I do some yoga stretches to get blood to my brain. Then, I meditate for at least five minutes. I try to do ten or fifteen minutes, then I do my gratitude practice where I write down at least three things I am grateful for. I set out to create positive energy at the beginning of the day so I can move through the day with complete gratitude. The Buddha talks about there being ten thousand joys and ten thousand sorrows. I know there is a lot of fucked-up stuff happening around the world, but there's a lot of joy as well, particularly in my own life. I want to focus on the good things so I am able to confront the injustices happening in the world. If I am grounded and grateful for all of the blessings I have, then I will be even stronger and will be able to deal with the negative. My gratitude practice is vitally important to me.

After that, I speak my desires as if they have already happened. When I was younger, a lot of them used to be focused on financial success because I was hungry and needed money. I have heard this a lot from teachers, but when people are trying to develop and manifest, a lot of their focus is usually on material needs or desires. I was in that place. Now that I feel like I have or have access to whatever I want materially for the most part, I am more focused on what I truly need to be happy. At this point in my life, a lot of the things I focus on are immaterial. For example, I will say, "I am a present, loving, easygoing husband and dad." That is what I want to embody because I can be a bit anal and high-stress. I understand there are aspects of myself that I need to work on. Who I am now allows me to embody whatever I'm feeling on a daily basis. I'm not passive about it, hoping one day I will be better. No, I want to be present, easygoing, loving, and chill every day. Those are the type of things a lot of my energy is going into now. I want my next book to have black food in it. I want this to have a positive impact globally. That is how I end my morning practices, speaking into existence what I see unfolding in my life.

G The last question I'd like to ask is for that person out there who may be saying, "I love vegetarian cuisine, and I want to be putting healthy whole foods on the table for my children, but I don't have the time. I'm juggling a full-time job and parenting, maybe while attaining higher education or cultivating a relationship with a significant other." A lot of people don't have cars or they spend a couple hours a day in traffic, in addition to all of these other commitments. Many people not only think it's much easier to throw something in the microwave or take a minute to whip up a sandwich, but sometimes it's all they have time for. What advice and tips would you give that person?

B That is a great question, and I need to recognize that there are people who have wildly different circumstances. The first thing I suggest is preparing the recipes that require more time and labor on the weekends. However, I also recognize that there are people who work seven days a week. They work their main job during the week and another job on the weekends. For me, this is why you can't talk about families feeding themselves without talking about the economy and the ways in which workers are so often exploited and underpaid. If you are not working a job that is paying you a livable wage, then of course you are going to have to get another job that will fill in those gaps. I believe that blaming working people for not working hard enough, when they work hard as shit but aren't being fairly compensated, is actually enriching corporations.

I think we have to recognize those realities around capitalism and the way it incentivizes a small group of people to hoard resources and not fairly compensate or give opportunities for ownership or profits to people who are actually putting in the work. That is one piece, but I think for the people who do have the time and space, meal planning is an important tool for healthful eating. I am not going to judge anyone. I think there is too much shaming against working class people who eat fast food or a lot of processed foods. I think those are connected, and yeah, if you are going from one job and rushing to the next one, of course grabbing a burger can be quick and easy to fill your stomach. I feel like the idea that eating healthy is too expensive fails to recognize that it is actually pretty cheap if you think about buying grains, beans, and legumes in bulk. When you factor in the time that goes into making meals from scratch, some people would rather spend that hour making money. So often, I think when people are striving to eat more healthily, they see it as an individual endeavor. People say, "Yeah, I am going to eat more healthy," but I think they come across the barriers of time, cost, or labor. These are absolutely valid barriers for some people, and we need to address the reality of how those things play out in some people's lives. It may be costly for some people to buy fresh products when they live in certain communities that don't have a lot of those options. Even if their neighborhood does offer those options, they may be priced higher compared to affluent neighborhoods. So all of this is real, but I think one major thing is realizing that you don't have to do it alone. Think about healthy eating as a community endeavor.

Many people are trying to figure out how to wean themselves off of the standard American diet and eat a more plant-based diet with fruits and vegetables. Having a support group and a community of people to do it with you makes it a little easier. Instead of going to the farmer's market alone and buying all your fresh foods, imagine that you gather half a dozen friends, family members, or colleagues and pull all of your money together to collectively buy all the items from the farmer's market. Then, you can go back to someone's house and cook the dishes together. Say everybody makes one dish, then you will have six different dishes you can divvy among the group to freeze and eat throughout the workweek. Doing this with a group of people is fun, and it builds community. By sharing your resources, you have the opportunity to have a bunch of home-cooked meals you can eat all week. Just that act alone hits on so many things: community-building and communal activities, to name a couple. We have to get out of this capitalistic mentality that perpetuates the idea that individualism is the only way you can become successful or resolve issues. Community is key.

JEAN DAVID NKOT
Pg. 268-269
WWW.GOLDPLANNER.ORG, 2020
© Jean David Nkot. Courtesy of the artist and Jack Bell Gallery, London

WHATEVER
I WANT,

I FEEL LIKE I CAN HAVE.

IF I HAVE A GOAL I WANT TO ACHIEVE, I PUT
IT OUT THERE, TAKE ACTIONABLE STEPS,
AND CREATE LONG-TERM AND SHORT-
TERM GOALS. IF I CAN'T GET IT, THEN
THAT MEANS I DON'T NEED TO HAVE IT."

ANTHONY

THO

JAMARI

MAS

JARRETT KEY
Warrior at Rest, 2020
© Jarrett Key.
Courtesy of the artist

GLENN You created an installation in collaboration with Dover Street Market and John Dominguez titled "NO COLOUR, MO' COLOUR," which examined stereotypes and human conditioning as it applies to race and color. Was there a specific point in your life when those questions and that concept began to arise in you, and were there layers of yourself that you could shed to further know the real you?

ANTHONY A lot of my practice deals with the concept of inherit identity and thinking about how much of you and what you deem valuable is comprised of history and your relationship to memory and family. A huge element of "NO COLOUR, MO' COLOUR" came from looking at my childhood and teenage years growing up in a Southern Baptist Christian home. A lot of the thoughts I carried were learned through my experiences in church because it was the only place I saw the collateral congregation of people and what that could produce in terms of spiritual movement, spiritual progression, success, and joy. A lot of that enabled me to understand that there were different things that were intertwined into the black experience and programming.

I did the project with John Dominguez because he invited me out, and it was through a collaboration with my publisher. But also, I thought about how the company itself signifies culture in many ways for fashion and art. It is indeed a very progressive space, and the collection was actually inspired by James Baldwin. It illuminates the relationship between mass media programming and the artist. How much of yourself can you see in the media until you start seeing either a lack or an abundance of confrontation? I thought it was interesting that I co-oped in these art and fashion spaces, but I rarely ever saw conversations that sparked socio-political discourse or identity politics, and it may be there, but it's ingrained in a certain code where it is presented through commerce in a pseudo fashion. You get the conversation, but it's a little bit softened because there is an exchange of finances happening. So for me, in that situation, I just wanted to have the most abrupt, aggressive conversation about politics and black identity, and I wanted to put them on display in an enterprise that doesn't stray away from those topics but, rather, sees the benefit in having those conversations around normal operations.

I would say the flashiness of it came from my mom raising me on Puff and Bad Boy. Biggie was a huge piece of my childhood, and seeing someone who was so heroic and creative be killed was tough. Then to see this type of Phoenix situation with Puffy coming up and doing what he needed to do to become a mogul with a sense of hope and joy was incredible. So it was all these different forms of acceptance that my family brought me up with, and when I came into the program as a child, they placed me in several institutions, forums, routines, and rituals so I wouldn't see the oppression and the demands society placed on me and my racial identity. They kept me in this nest of their processes and saved me in a way. I use church because of the coming of God. I think it goes in a simple loop, and everything is like an oasis, a part of a whole.

G Your practice has covered a wide terrain, from projects like "This Fragmented Stream of Consciousness" with Malik Kirkwood to *LAMB,* which is a combination of performance and literature that examines migrancy. I read in an interview with *Office Magazine* that during the creation of *LAMB,* you were "in the depths of depression." Can you speak about that time in your life, how that depression manifested, and how you were able to continue working?

A I think challenges, disasters, and crises are interesting because they bring out the truth in yourself and others. It can be protested, but there is an element of fact, myth, and truth that always arises in emergencies, and for me, that book ended up being one of the truths I needed to tell. The reason I had such an intense relationship with depression at the time was because my aunt passed away. My aunt was the reason I had a studio practice. She gave me a room in her home to build my visual language and never shied away from telling me she was there to take on whatever I was going through. When I lost her, it was like losing my friend, my mentor, and my counselor. She was my spiritual guide, my ancestral connection, and I felt like I lost that.

A month later, I lost my uncle who was her brother, then in the same week, I lost my cousin. A month later, I was in a car accident in a Lyft, which was crazy. So there was a lot of breaking down, and I thought that time was interesting because I was broken down in ways I never thought I could be. I was angry, upset, and depressed, so I decided to make a piece and write about it. There was so much pressure built up; it was like an airbag. Those events were my airbags. So when my airbag was released, it kept releasing, and after a while, it lost its intensity. I had my airbag go off about four times in the span of two months, with the last hit being my fiancée. She moved back to Europe so we ended our engagement, and I was alone.

I remember there were some days I needed to grieve my aunt's death, and I built those wooden cases. When I would grieve, I would make those, and it kind of reminded me of carpentry and Jesus. My aunt was talking to me still, and when I couldn't talk to my significant other, I would go within, and that became my physical safe space. The book as a concept became my safe space, and once I got to the finish line of publishing it, I didn't feel anything. It felt like I had lost the book that I had packed so much into. My spirit was like, "OK, we need to release this because we need to save ourselves, but if we don't execute, we won't know what is on the other side. This is going to help us." The cultures of the game were excited I finished the book, but I had just made it through so many stages of abandonment that I didn't know if the book would've meant the same thing if those people hadn't departed. So then I started looking at what the book really meant. It allowed the people I photographed to open up and blossom so they could see themselves. Also, the book was heavily talked about in politics and the media, but I felt that localizing and internalizing it within the community would be the best way to honor the other side. It ended up being my anchor, savior, and labor force all at the same time.

G You've also spoken publicly about battling depression and anxiety as a teenager, even having suicidal ideations during that period. You've also written about attending therapy via a post on your Instagram page. When did you begin going to therapy, and has it assisted with your personal growth and healing?

A My most official connection and relationship with therapy was about a year ago. All my attempts before were a lust for peace, and it was a peace I knew I couldn't create on my own due to a lack of resources. I had a thousand broken pieces, and the community I was in tried its best to glue them back together. Every time I got with the community I loved, I noticed that people were hurting. It's not that we are not professionals and can't help each other, but rather, we were all dealing with something so we couldn't effectively help the next person. We couldn't use each other to fill our cups because we were all coming from a place of negativity or lack. It made me really think about healing and how I needed to own the process.

With my work, I spend a lot of time writing proposals and grants. This account needs to see me, so I need to like seven photos on their Instagram so they know I am aware of their presence and they can follow my work—the tricks of the trade. As a visual artist, you're often just playing the game, so being seen online has become a very conceptual and creative process. I began to wonder if I was building that same process for my healing, and I realized I wasn't. I was treating my artistic practice and ability to be seen as phase one while juggling everything else. I said to myself, *If I am broken by the time these people see me, then I'll have nothing for them, so let me get equally creative in this realm before I try to present my vibe to somebody.*

I got very aggressive in getting my concepts out, aggressive with love. I just got very creative about finding therapy and the people I needed to help me out and get me to the place I needed to be. I reached out, put everything on the table, and found a very beautiful woman in New York. She ended up getting back to me, and it was a done deal. The beautiful thing about it was it allowed me to see the hurt in my family. I started painting in 2014, a few installations, nothing big. Everything was still in color, then I started shooting photography, and my mother was diagnosed with cancer. I went into my catalog and was like, "Again, I am creating all of these vibes for people to see and love me, but if my mom passes away, I don't own any photos of her." I literally had none on my camera or iPhone, so if she passed, I'd have to go to somebody else's photobook and ask them if I could have a picture. I felt like I was not applying that same creativity into harvesting images of my family.

So, I started doing photography, and it revealed the inner workings of my family that were ripped and torn. I started to be a little more forgiving with the time I was giving to others. I took ownership, and I hope those pictures can serve as a testament to my dedication. So again, I just relate photography to therapy, as it allowed me to see my family. When I started therapy, I started to see the womb, so the photos broke the mold for me. Instead of my family being a concept of the hood or poverty, I can now see them for them. Therapy made me dig a little bit deeper.

I AM OWNING
MY

TIME
AND
TRAUMAS

SO I CAN BE A FULL
PERSON.

277

My photography shows my mom alone because she was a single parent taking care of two kids. Therapy allowed me to see that not only was she a single mother, but she was also a woman. All my communication at the time was built around how to interface with a romantic partner. I had a hard time communicating and connecting with a woman. The more I saw my mom as the matriarch, the more I was able to understand the complexity of my relationship with women. To connect to the woman I wanted to connect to, I had to connect to the womb and the things that were broken so I didn't recreate the same trauma. Therapy gave me another tool and weapon to heal myself and view my mom as a leader and a woman with needs. I am her son. What does it mean to be one of the more consistent figures in her life? What does it mean to take on that role when she never really had that before?

It goes into my romantic partnerships and my relationship with my half-brother. Again, in the past, my therapy was alcohol, depression, and suicidal thoughts. I never followed through, but those things definitely impaired my health. It is a beautiful thing to have therapy in your life, but sometimes you need money to access it. The parameters of my life made it an affordable tool to bring myself healing. It has helped me see so much with my camera and paintbrush or any installation. It helps me see with such clarity. It made work, images, people, and myself softer in terms of proximity, acceptance, and comfort. Things I thought I was entitled to, like family, DNA, and blood, seemed arbitrary; I wanted to master them. Then, I understood that my family is my first gift, and to have any success, I needed to cherish and honor my gifts the same way I cherish and honor my work.

If I cherish my work in the public eye without cherishing my family or the things that mean the most to me, how much of a success am I? Then I started thinking, *What does success mean to me, and what does getting on mean for me?* Now I am owning my time and traumas so I can be a full person. When I meet people, I like to be present. I like to look in their eyes and hug them.

I love contact; a lot of my work involves contact. I love physicality; I love being close. In my personal life, I love to have everyone together, then I go three months or longer before calling my mom because I am out here hustling. So for me, it just really gave me principles to live by and a foundation, an activity and identity, and it made my family a priority alongside the other things in my life. It is full circle.

G Prayer is a word that appears often in your practice. What does prayer mean to you, and what role does it serve in your life?

A I was reading a book by Malcolm X, and toward the end, he spoke about prayer twice. The first time he converted to Islam, he talked about the discipline of praying to the rug. It was a different experience because his context was against the conversation of whiteness. The whole agenda of the religion is to go against something he didn't want to exist. So today, we went to the Haji, prayed in Arabic, and listened to each other. We had our palms up, and today, something about the prayer was relaxing. What I enjoy about prayer is that it is something to lean into. It is just as strong as my work, which is built up through these constant fibers. It goes back to rituals, to practicing so much you get to the point where you must lean into it and evaluate the firmness like a mattress. When I am stressed out, I can find interaction and be relieved that this thing, my work, has come forth through the grace of God.

Prayers have been an anchor, and I believe God gave me the gift of oration. Being able to speak and write well has been the crux of the last two or three months with COVID and the civil rights movement happening. I just had to be as creative and radical as I would be for everything else in my life. So in the mosque, when he gets on his knees and prays to God, he says, "I want to be that much more vulnerable, forward, present, creative, that much more conceptual about how I talk to my father." It is very fulfilling. I wish I could give you a mystifying explanation of what it means to me, but prayer can be anything. I think it simply allows you to alienate yourself from the normal and bring forth transcendence. Our artworks and practices are a form of prayer. It doesn't always have to be done on the knees or in the temple. If you can sit in front of a camera or a blank space and make something exist, you are embodying the true essence of God when He created the Earth.

BRAD OGBONNA

Pg. 279
Gas Station (Dakar, Senegal), 2019
© Brad Ogbonna.
Courtesy of the artist

JOR

"WATTS"

DAN

WATSON

GLENN You've spoken about growing up in Jamaica, Queens. Can you speak about that neighborhood and what it was like when you were a kid?

WATTS I was born in 1979 in Jamaica, Queens, and was raised in Rochdale Village. I grew up when crime and the crack epidemic were hitting New York hard. I remember playing outside and seeing these crack vials everywhere. It was just normal New York life. At that time, it was all I really knew.

G You've stated that your introduction to art was through skateboarding. What was it like being into skateboarding in that neighborhood at that time?

W I started skateboarding when I was ten, and I remember nobody was skating back then. I would skate by myself, read skateboarding magazines, like *Thrasher* and *Big Brother,* then go out and try to do the tricks. I learned everything on my own. My parents started taking me to this skate park in the Bronx called Mullaly Park. That was the first time I saw Puerto Rican kids with my skin tone skating, but I didn't join a skate crew until high school, when my parents moved me to Long Island. Before that, it was me, the magazines, and ratchet skate parks I used to visit on "skate dates" in New York.

G Would anyone ever call you out about skateboarding, saying it's a white guy's thing?

W Probably, but I don't remember much from that time. I was never an outcast, though. I went to Richmond Hill, which is a school for gifted kids, and I was always pretty popular. In kindergarten, I was the only black kid in school, so while I was living in an all-black community, I went to a school with only white kids. Looking back, that's probably the time I was introduced to skating. When I got to high school, people called me out a bit, but they would just call me things like "Arrested Development" because in their eyes, I was a little eccentric. I was never teased for the skateboarding, but since an early age, people would say, "You sound like a white boy." At that time, I didn't even know what that meant.

G Your art-centered Instagram page, @Love.Watts, has over 2 million followers. Can you speak about the period of time after you saw some success with your page? Did you have a huge vision for the brand when you created it?

W It's funny because I'm still going through that period. I have a bunch of followers, but I had a life before I created the Love Watts page, and these followers don't translate to real people in my head. I have a ton of followers, but I don't look at it in that way. I'm still trying to build my brand. I've had some success and have been able to travel all over, but I've never been convinced that I'm poppin'.

283

Instagram is just one way to build brand awareness, so my focus now has shifted to getting my Instagram followers to engage on my own platform, which is completely regulated by me without restrictions or censorship. There hasn't been a defining moment where "I've made it," and things became different. I'm from a different generation, and I don't equate clout to success. The key is to convert the clout into cash because the clout doesn't pay the bills.

G You've done a variety of different things with Love Watts, including "In Color" with Instagram, in which you had a pop-up art gallery showcasing black artistry at The Watts Empowerment Center in Watts, California. You've also created The Love Watts Foundation, which is a charity dedicated to supporting art programs for inner city youth all over the country. What role do you see art playing in the development and ultimate success of young people growing up in the inner city?

W That's an amazing question. To me, art is a luxury, and getting inner city youth to love and appreciate art is a sign of freedom.

Many of these kids had never seen fine art up close. We were at The Watts Empowerment Center, and being in that environment was a bit of a shocker for me. I knew what the neighborhoods were like, but to go there and bring that experience to those kids, to see the looks on their faces and to hear how appreciative the mothers were was everything to me. It's definitely one of my callings.

I'm starting a new initiative that is doing the same type of work we did with the "In Color" series. The plan is to go to cities across America and bring the fine art experience to various communities, opening children's minds to think a little differently about art. Instead of getting them on a yellow bus and shuttling them to a museum, we'll bring the museum right to their doorstep. Sometimes it's the only light switch you need.

G Do you have any advice for black men out there who are pursuing their dreams?

W Keep fighting through. When you're focused on something you have to do, you can't give up. I think the hardest thing is figuring out what you should be focused on, and sometimes that can take years all on its own. It took me about thirty-five years to get to where I am today. I went through a series of different stages in my life that all made sense at the time, and they all led me to what I'm doing now. The only common denominator is that I worked hard at everything I did. I always stayed positive, and I know that sounds cliché, but I learned early on that if I kept a smile on my face and kept working hard, good things would come to me. It may sound simple, but that's where my success lies.

THE ONLY COMMON DENOMINATOR IS THAT I <u>WORKED</u> <u>HARD</u> AT EVERYTHING I DID. I ALWAYS STAYED POSITIVE, AND I KNOW THAT SOUNDS CLICHÉ, BUT I LEARNED EARLY ON THAT IF I KEPT A <u>SMILE</u> ON MY FACE AND KEPT WORKING HARD, GOOD THINGS WOULD COME TO <u>ME.</u>

THANK YOU

TO ALL OF THE CONTRIBUTORS AND
SUPPORTERS OF THERE'S LIGHT.
WITHOUT YOUR HONESTY, TRUST AND
GENEROSITY, THIS PROJECT WOULD
NOT BE POSSIBLE.

THANK YOU TO THE ARTISTS
AND GALLERIES WHO ASSISTED IN THE
CREATION OF THIS BOOK, AND TO
THE BRILLIANT TEAM AT PAPRIKA WHO
SHARED THIS VISION WITH ME.

THANK YOU TO LYRIC AND KATHLEEN
FOR THEIR METICULOUS EDITING,
AND TO MY PARTNER AALIYAH FOR HER
COLLABORATION AND INSIGHT.

THERE'S LIGHT
IS DEDICATED TO VIRGIL ABLOH.
HIS PASSION, CREATIVITY AND KINDNESS
WAS AND IS AN INSPIRATION
TO US ALL.

Photograph by
Devin Timothy Nelson & Olu Femi.

Glenn Lutz (b. 1988, Upland, CA) is an author and
conceptual artist whose work examines themes
related to identity, spirituality, mental health, and
race. Using a wide range of mediums including
publications, curation, performance, works on paper,
video sculpture, and musical compositions under the
moniker Zenn Lu, his practice's central concerns are
exploration, storytelling, investigation, and activism.

You can follow his work at glennlutz.com and on
Instagram at @glenn_lutz.

CPSIA information can be obtained
at www.ICGtesting.com
Printed in the USA
LVHW072123181122
733522LV00014B/965